Demography, Education, and the Workforce

Demography, Education, and the Workforce

ROBERT I. LERMAN
AND
STEPHANIE RIEGG CELLINI

GREENWOOD GUIDES TO BUSINESS AND ECONOMICS
Wesley B. Truitt, Series Editor

GREENWOOD PRESS
Westport, Connecticut • London

Library of Congress Cataloging-in-Publication Data

Lerman, Robert I.
   Demography, education, and the workforce/Robert I. Lerman
and Stephanie Riegg Cellini.
       p. cm.—(Greenwood guides to business and economics)
   Includes index.
   ISBN 978-0-313-35219-5 (hbk. : alk. paper)—ISBN 978-0-313-35220-1 (ebook)
   1. Population. 2. Population aging. 3. Labor supply. 4. Education.
5. Emigration and immigration. I. Riegg, Stephanie K., 1977–
II. Title.
   HB871.L476   2009
   331.11′43—dc22   2009005395

British Library Cataloguing in Publication Data is available.

Library of Congress Catalog Card Number: 2009005395
ISBN: 978-0-313-35219-5
ISSN: 1559-2367

First published in 2009

Greenwood Press, 88 Post Road West, Westport, CT 06881
An imprint of Greenwood Publishing Group, Inc.
www.greenwood.com

Printed in the United States of America

The paper used in this book complies with the
Permanent Paper Standard issued by the National
Information Standards Organization (Z39.48–1984).

10   9   8   7   6   5   4   3   2   1

To our spouses,
Ariella Lerman and Lorenzo Cellini,
for their love and support

Contents

Series Foreword

Scanning the pages of the newspaper on any given day, you'll find headlines like the following.

"OPEC points to supply chains as cause of price hikes"
"Business groups warn of danger of takeover proposals"
"U.S. durable goods orders jump 3.3%"
"Dollar hits two-year high versus yen"
"Credibility of WTO at stake in trade talks"
"U.S. GDP growth slows while Fed fears inflation growth"

If this seems like gibberish to you, then you are in good company. To most people, the language of economics is mysterious, intimidating, impenetrable. But with economic forces profoundly influencing our daily lives, being familiar with the ideas and principles of business and economics is vital to our welfare. From fluctuating interest rates to rising gasoline prices to corporate misconduct to the vicissitudes of the stock market to the rippling effects of protests and strikes overseas or natural disasters closer to home, "the economy" is not an abstraction. As Robert Duvall, president and CEO of the National Council on Economic Education, has forcefully argued: "Young people in our country need to know that economic education is not an option. Economic literacy is a vital skill, just as vital as reading literacy."[1]

Understanding economics is a skill that will help you interpret current events playing out on a global scale or in your checkbook, ultimately helping you make wiser choices about how you manage your financial resources—today and tomorrow.

It is the goal of this series, *Greenwood Guides to Business and Economics*, to promote economic literacy and improve economic decision making. All books in the series are written for the general reader; high school and college student; or the business manager, entrepreneur, or graduate student in business and economics looking for a handy refresher. They have been written by experts in their respective fields for nonexpert readers. The approach throughout is at a "basic" level to maximize understanding and to demystify how our business-driven economy really works.

Each book in the series is an essential guide to the topic of that volume, providing an introduction to its respective subject area. The series as a whole constitutes a library of information, up-to-date data, definitions of terms, and resources, covering all aspects of economic activity. Volumes feature such elements as timelines, glossaries, and examples and illustrations that bring the concepts to life and present them in historical and cultural context.

The selection of the titles and their authors has been the work of an Editorial Advisory Board, whose members are the following: Alan Carsrud, Florida International University; Alan Reynolds, Cato Institute; Wesley Truitt, Pepperdine University; Walter E. Williams, George Mason University; and Charles Wolf Jr., RAND Corporation.

As series editor, I served as chairman of the Editorial Advisory Board and want to express my appreciation to each of these distinguished individuals for their dedicated service in helping bring this important series to reality.

The volumes in the series are as follows:

The Corporation by Wesley B. Truitt, School of Public Policy, Pepperdine University

Entrepreneurship by Alan L. Carsrud, Florida International University, and Malin Brännback, Åbo Akademi University

Globalization by Donald J. Boudreaux, George Mason University

Income and Wealth by Alan Reynolds, Cato Institute

Money by Mark Dobeck and Euel Elliott, University of Texas at Dallas

The National Economy by Bradley A. Hansen, University of Mary Washington

The Stock Market by Rik W. Hafer, Southern Illinois University–Edwardsville, and Scott E. Hein, Texas Tech University

Demography, Education, and the Workforce by Robert I. Lerman, American University and Urban Institute; and Stephanie Riegg Cellini, George Washington University

Energy by Joseph M. Dukert, Center for Strategic and International Studies

Real Estate by Mark F. Dobeck, Cleveland State University

Special thanks to our original editor at Greenwood, Nick Philipson, for conceiving the idea of the series and for sponsoring it within Greenwood Press, and many thanks to our current senior editor, Jeff Olson, for skillfully steering the continuation of the series.

The overriding purpose of each of these books and the series as a whole is, as Walter Williams so aptly put it, to "push back the frontiers of ignorance."

Wesley B. Truitt, Series Editor

NOTE

1. Quoted in Gary H. Stern, "Do We Know Enough about Economics?" *The Region*, Federal Reserve Bank of Minneapolis, December 1998.

Acknowledgments

This book would not have been possible without the encouragement, comments, suggestions, and hard work of many people. We thank our excellent research assistants: Faith Fried, Erin O'Keefe, and Stephanie Stone at George Washington University, and Aneil Baron at the Urban Institute for all of their hard work. Comments and suggestions from Bryan Boulier, Dylan Conger, and Hal Wolman were quite helpful. We especially appreciate the patience and many helpful suggestions of our editors, Jeff Olson and Wesley B. Truitt at Greenwood Press. Both Jeff and Wesley worked closely with us from the time the book was conceived until its completion.

One

Introduction

Population patterns and trends play central roles in the ways economies develop, social life functions, income is distributed, labor markets operate, and government programs are run. *Demography* is the main field examining the size and composition of populations, life course patterns affecting populations, and the implications for the social and economic environment. Formally, demography is defined as the statistical study of human populations, but it is more commonly described as the study of births, deaths, migration, and immigration. Further, the term demography is often used synonymously with population patterns—a convention we adopt throughout this book.

Although demography does not *determine* a nation's destiny, private and public actors should recognize that demographic trends greatly influence and are influenced by markets and institutions, including governments, schools, and families. This book provides a nontechnical guide to help citizens—whether managers, workers, students, retirees, or government officials—understand demographic trends in the United States and their implications for the labor market and for education.

Theory and data have long demonstrated close links between demography, wages, and living standards. In the 18th century, political economist Thomas Malthus famously posited that increases in living standards are offset by rapid population growth, leaving income per person unchanged: only during population declines would wages rise (Malthus and Gilbert 1999). Consistent with the theory, the scarcity of labor that accompanied massive population losses due to the "Black Death" of the 14th century led to sharp increases in wages— 100 percent in some regions (Pamuk 2007). As population growth resumed over the next three centuries, wages fell back toward their pre-plague levels in some countries. However, in others new technologies prevented sharp declines in wages, in effect disproving Malthus's theories. While Malthus's pessimism was understandable, given the low living standards he observed in his time, the experiences of the last 200 years have further chipped away at Malthus's claim. As population has grown, technological change and investments in knowledge and physical capital have made dramatic jumps in wages and incomes possible.

Modern economic growth theories focus less on population growth and more on improvements in technology, along with expansions in investments in physical and human capital (Solow 1956; Romer 1990). Human capital—or education and training—plays a particularly important role. Indeed, while the level of population growth may affect the size of the economy, it has no long-term impact on income per person. Innovations—often spurred by educational investments—are central, as are the property right regimes that allow entrepreneurs to take full advantage of technology. In addition, education, training, and health care allow workers to raise their long-term productivity, wages, and living standards. Given that *declines* in population growth have taken place alongside the substantial growth in incomes in industrial countries in the last decades, the Malthusian view looks increasingly irrelevant. However, this is not to say that population trends play an insignificant role in the determinants of wages, incomes, and public policies.

Perhaps the most well-known, broadly discussed, and policy-relevant demographic trend is the baby-boom bulge in the decade after the end of World War II. The cohort associated with the jump in births in the late 1940s through the early 1960s filled elementary and secondary schools in the 1950s and 1960s; crowded colleges and the job market for young workers in the 1970s; expanded the prime-age workforce of the 1980s, 1990s, and early 2000s; and will substantially increase the number of retirees in 2010 through 2030. The baby boom, together with the subsequent decline in births (from 4.3 million in 1961 to 3.1 million in 1973) and rising life expectancy, are now leading to the aging of the U.S. population. The result is a declining ratio of workers to the elderly. This demographic trend, combined with the rapid growth in health spending on the elderly, is leading to massive growth in projected budgets for Social Security, Medicare, and Medicaid. The proportion of the nation's income required to pay for these three programs for older individuals is likely to double from about 8 percent of Gross Domestic Product (GDP) to 14.5 percent by 2030 and 18.6 percent by 2050 (Congressional Budget Office 2007). Spending on these federal programs would jump from 44 percent of federal spending today to 75 percent in 2030 and 96 percent in 2050, assuming federal taxes remain at their long-term average (nearly 19 percent of GDP). To afford these expansions and all other functions of the federal government without massive deficits, tax rates on workers and employers would have to rise by nearly 50 percent of current taxes. State outlays and taxes are projected to increase as well, since states pay over 40 percent of Medicaid outlays. State spending on Medicaid long-term care expenditures alone are projected to rise from $51.5 billion in 2008 to $115.6 billion in 2027 (Shostak and London 2008). These increases would lower net wages, expand the gap between what employers pay and what workers earn, and potentially lower economic activity in the formal, tax-reporting sector of the economy.

While these demographic trends are central factors associated with expected spending growth on U.S. health and retirement programs, they are not by themselves responsible for the added spending, budget deficits, and/or massive tax increases. Policy decisions matter as well. Public policy changes can at least partly offset the added eligibility for government benefits generated by demographic trends. For example, one policy change that could partly offset the aging-related additional government spending is to index Social Security benefits to life expectancy (Shoven and Godi 2008). Instead of the percentage of people qualifying for Social Security and Medicare rising from 12 percent today to 20 percent in 2050, a life expectancy adjustment in 2004 would limit the increase to 17 percent of the population. Other examples of policy changes that can alter budgetary and economic outcomes include changes in reimbursements for medical procedures and requiring high-income elderly to pay for a higher share of their health insurance under Medicare.

Adaptations to demographic changes in the private sphere can also influence economic and social developments. Firms may respond to the increased availability of older workers by altering their promotion and compensation policies or by learning how to use older workers more effectively. As employment options for older workers improve, more may delay retirement and thus offset the impact of population aging on government spending and taxes. At the same time, the upcoming decline in the percent of 25- to 54-year-old workers is likely to encourage firms to draw leaders from nontraditional sources and to undertake increases in training.

Population aging is one of many demographic trends that are exerting major impacts on the U.S. economy, workers, employers, social relations, educational systems, and public policy. Shifts in family and household composition, marriage and divorce, the living arrangements of children, internal migration, and immigration from abroad are among the other significant trends in demography that interact with the economy. The impacts flow in two directions. Internal migration, or migration within a country, for example, can affect the availability of workers, especially college-educated workers, and thus economic activity across regions. Conversely, the regional and/or urban patterns of economic growth no doubt influence internal migration. Employment and welfare policies might well influence marriage and divorce, since marriages may be less likely to last or to take place at all if the earnings of low-skill men add little to a family's income. At the same time, if men choose to remain single instead of marrying, the decline in the married share of the male population may lower their commitment to the labor force and lead to lower productivity and earnings.

The complex interactions between economic incentives, social mores, and demography are embedded in many issues of concern to Americans. Sometimes, as with the baby boom's impact on Social Security, the role of demography is widely appreciated and well known. In other cases, such as the effects of the inflow of low-educated immigrants on poverty rates, the public is less informed about the impact of demographic changes. But, researchers and the media are increasingly taking account of the impact of demography on a wide range of issues. Findings about the nature, causes, and consequences of demographic trends are emerging from studies undertaken by economists, sociologists, historians, public policy scholars, and demographers.

THE BOOK'S PRIMARY GOALS

This book highlights some of the most important demographic research from the last few decades and explores its intersection with the field of labor economics. As labor economists ourselves, we focus our attention on how emerging and past demographic patterns shape the U.S. job market and education system. We hope employers, educators, and other readers with strong interests in education and labor market issues will especially benefit from the book by expanding their knowledge about the linkages between demographic trends, what they see happening today, and what they expect for the future. Our intention is not to develop new findings, but rather to describe four major demographic trends in the U.S. and explore their consequences for the U.S. labor force and education system. We devote chapters to each of the following trends.

- The aging of the U.S. population and the populations of several other countries, in the context of national and international demographic shifts.
- Changes in how U.S. families and households are organized, partly as the result of declining marriage rates, rising rates of nonmarital births, cohabitation, and one-parent families.
- Ups and downs of both legal and illegal international migration flows into the United States and how immigration has altered and continues to affect the size, education, and ethnic patterns of the U.S. population.
- Shifts in the urban and regional population of the United States, especially the role of migration within the United States.

These trends no doubt overlap in complex ways. For example, international immigration may lower wage rates, which in turn hurts the earnings of low-skill men, making them less likely to marry and have a stable family life. The final chapter concentrates on the nature of the interactions among the trends examined in the prior four chapters.

In examining these patterns and trends, the book draws on studies by demographers but also by economists, sociologists, and historians. We rely extensively on graphs to illustrate, while avoiding an excessively technical approach. Each chapter highlights similarities and differences by race and ethnicity, by sex, and by children and adults. Often, we explore emerging patterns in other countries and ask whether the United States is following international patterns or is the exception.

A PREVIEW OF KEY DEMOGRAPHIC TRENDS

We begin in Chapter 2 by first describing how the world's population has evolved and then turning to a close look at recent and future trends in the United States. Viewed from a long-term and world perspective, the last 500 years, and especially the last 100 years, have been exceptional. Over the 1st through the 10th century, the world's population barely increased and rose little through 1750. Then, led by rising living standards that came with industrialization and declining death rates in European and North American countries, the number of people began increasing more rapidly, culminating in a jump from about 2 billion to 5 billion people between 1930 and 1990. Recently, population growth has been declining in high-, middle- and low-income countries, in spite of big increases in life expectancy. By 2050, the world's population is expected to stabilize, if not decline, for the second half of the century.

The decline in birth rates and increase in life expectancy are leading to the aging of populations, from Korea and China in Asia to Italy, Spain, and Germany in Western Europe. The United States is experiencing population aging as well, albeit at a slower pace than in other high-income countries. Chapter 2 presents a detailed picture of these trends and then examines some of the consequences. Not only is labor force growth expected to decline, but older workers will be nearly the only source of growth. Older workers are likely to become increasingly active in the job market and more in demand over the next decades. Schools in the United States will experience a slowdown in the growth of the student population. Moreover, as older people become a larger voting bloc, citizen support for high amounts of education spending may decline, forcing schools to limit their spending and to not expect the types of dollar increases they have experienced in recent years.

In Chapter 3, the focus is on the changing structure of families and households. Here, the demographic trends are both a cause and an effect. Social changes in the role of women, in the occupational structure of modern economies, and in the policies government pursues have all influenced the way people organize themselves into families and households. At the same time, the declines in marriage and birth rates and the rising number of older people who live alone affect work patterns, government spending, and education policies. Few social trends have been as controversial as demographic shifts in parenthood (toward single-parents and father absence) and marriage. Some see enormous costs to society in general and taxpayers in particular resulting from the rise in single-parenthood and decline in marriage. Others note that the changes are benign and in any event the natural consequences of equality for women in the family and in the labor market. The chapter examines the nature of family change and size of the changes; for example, are the declines in marriage a shift away from marriage over one's lifetime or simply a delay in the age of marriage?

Like population aging, changes in family structure caused significant consequences for the job market and education. Perhaps the most important change is the dramatic rise in the share of women in the workforce. Looking to the future, the large and rising number of children growing up in single-parent families, many of which have limited incomes, is likely to complicate the job of the educational system. Employers may experience less stability among male workers because of the declining share of who are married.

The number of people in a country or area within a country depends not only on births and deaths, but also on net migration. For the United States, the most controversial component of migration is international—people moving into the United States. Chapter 4 takes a look at this aspect of migration, while Chapter 5 examines migration patterns and trends within the United States. The chapters present the relevant demographic trends along with their implications for the labor market and education. Again, causal chains run in both directions. Migrants come to the United States as jobs expand, implying that demography is an outcome of a growing and/or high wage economy. At the same time, high and rising numbers of immigrants increase the supply of workers, potentially lowering wages for some groups of workers. The data on immigration into the United States reveal dramatic increases in the late 19th century and early 20th century, followed by reductions in the middle of the 20th century, and rapid growth in immigration in the last few decades. The sources of immigration have shifted dramatically as well, from Europe in the 1880s through 1920s to Mexico, other Latin American countries, and Asia in the 1980s and 1990s. Despite large swings in immigration, the impacts on the labor market are far from obvious. One reason is that, while immigrants add to the supply of workers, they also contribute to the demand for workers. Some generate innovations that attract consumers from the rest of the world. Others simply use their earnings and assets to invest and consume. What is clear is that high levels of immigration lead to increases in the number and diversity of students. Chapter 4 discusses the serious challenges that the education system has faced and continues to face, especially in educating the children of low-income immigrants.

Although less controversial than international immigration, the movement of people within the United States is of greater magnitude. Between 1995 and 2000, about 22 million people moved from one state to another. Chapter 5 details the trends in internal migration and examines their implications. The willingness of Americans to move, especially in response to the labor market demands, is often cited as part of U.S. exceptionalism. Between the Civil War and the middle of the 20th century, the dominant pattern of migration was toward Western states and away from Southern states. By the 1960s, Southern states were beginning to experience net inflows of migrants, while people were leaving the Northeast. Within metropolitan areas, the mobility of people largely involved leaving central cities and moving to the suburbs. In recent years, central cities have begun to attract young people but have not reclaimed their previous shares of the populations in their respective metropolitan areas.

Like international immigration and the other demographic trends, mobility within the United States is both a cause and effect of developments within the labor market and education. People often move to where the jobs are, but companies sometimes move to where the people are, especially when the people are talented and highly skilled. Recent evidence (Moretti 2008) suggests that internal migration may alter conventional interpretations of the rising wage gap between college graduates and high school graduates. Because college graduates increasingly concentrate in metropolitan areas with high and rising living expenses, the rise in their living standards relative to those of high school graduates has been much lower than prior estimates suggest. This research is a good example of how demographic factors can play central roles in broader economic phenomena.

In the following chapters, we review the demographic patterns that have shaped the last century of U.S. history, as well as those that will shape the next. Ever evolving and interacting, changes in births, deaths, migration, and immigration are destined to have profound implications for our workforce and education systems in the years to come. From employment and earnings to academic achievement and attainment, from business considerations to policy implications, the this book explores the many ways that demography affects our world, our workforce, our children, and our future.

REFERENCES

Congressional Budget Office. 2007. *The Long-term Budget Outlook.* Congress of the United States. http://www.cbo.gov/ftpdocs/88xx/doc8877/12-13-LTBO.pdf.

Malthus, Thomas Robert, and Geoffrey Gilbert. 1999. *T. R. Malthus: An Essay on the Principle of Population.* Oxford, United Kingdom: Oxford World's Classics, Oxford University Press.

Moretti, Enrico. 2008. "Real Wage Inequality." Working Paper No. 14370. Cambridge, MA: National Bureau of Economic Research.

Pamuk, Sevket. 2007. "The Black Death and Origins of the 'Great Divergence' across Europe." *European Review of Economic History* II: 289–317.

Romer, Paul. 1990. "Endogenous Technological Change." *Journal of Political Economy* 98 (5, pt. 2): S71–S102.

Shostak, Daniel, and Paul London. 2008. *State Medicaid Expenditures for Long-term Care, 2008–2027.* Paul A. London and Associates and Strategic Affairs Forecasting. http://www.ahip.org/content/default.aspx?docid=24597.

Shoven, John, and Gopi Shah Godi. 2008. "Adjusting Government Policies for Age Inflation." Working Paper 14231. Cambridge, MA: National Bureau of Economic Research.

Solow, Robert. 1956. "A Contribution to the Theory of Economic Growth." *Quarterly Journal of Economics* 70: 65–94.

Two

Population Patterns, the Life Cycle, and Aging

Population growth has long conjured up images of the crowding of the planet, of a world rapidly running out of natural resources, of tragic environmental damage, and of mass starvation. In 1968, Paul Ehrlich, a Stanford biology professor, published *The Population Bomb* and foresaw scenarios in which the world would be unable to prevent hundreds of millions of people from starving to death in the 1970s and 1980s. A few years later, the Club of Rome published *The Limits of Growth* (Meadows et al. 1972), a report that cited alarming population trends that were leading to desperate shortages of arable land and many resources. These forecasts wildly missed the mark, as rising food production actually reduced world hunger, despite increases in the world population. Today, the most common long-term predictions by demographers are for slower population growth and potentially even depopulation, as argued by Ben Wattenberg in his 2004 book, aptly named *Fewer.*

The U.S. picture is mixed—a marked slowdown in natural population growth, coupled with rising amounts of immigration, and resulting in slow but continuing growth. This pattern is becoming increasingly characteristic for the world as a whole, but differences among countries in population growth are the most notable trends taking place today and for the foreseeable future.

The enormous forecasting errors of the last few decades should make us humble about our ability to predict population growth accurately for the coming decades. Still, anyone formulating private or public policies for a future economy must consider which outcomes look most likely for population growth and what do these outcomes imply. Will the United States have too few workers to support an aging population? Will the job market tighten and cause rising wages, as the number of 25- to 54-year-olds stagnates or declines? Or will the seemingly inexorable growth of immigration and trade limit wage growth and assure an adequate labor supply? Will the education system be able to respond sensibly to changes in the size and mix of students? How will the structure of goods and services demanded by an aging population affect the types of occupations in demand? The answers to these and many other questions depend importantly on demographic developments, mainly in the United States, but also in the world at large.

The task of this chapter is to present what we know about the past and what we expect about the future with regard to the size and mix of the U.S. population. To place U.S. population developments in context, we begin with a brief review of past and future demographic patterns in the world as a whole. Next, we describe in more detail demographic trends in the United States, including births, deaths, and the life cycles of selected birth cohorts. Third, we consider the impacts of these trends on what has been and what is expected to take place in the U.S. job market and what are the likely and most desirable responses by key public and private actors. The fourth section looks closely at how demographic developments are affecting and will affect the U.S. education system.

THE EXPANSION AND LEVELING OFF OF THE WORLD'S POPULATION

Populations evolve in dynamic ways. If births rise unexpectedly in one year, not only will the population increase today, but the number of women at childbearing ages will increase 18 to 45 years later, setting off a likely further increase in births. Declining mortality at older ages will increase a country's population size but lower its birth rate simply because a smaller share of the population will be at childbearing age. Since declines in mortality take place slowly, the aging of the population will generally lower the population growth rate. Immigration may account for little growth (and no natural growth) in one year, but the continuing inflow of migrants may raise natural growth in the future by increasing a nation's overall birth rate if immigrants have above-average fertility rates. Thus, a complex combination of past, present, and future fertility and mortality rates will determine a nation's population, age structure, and growth.

To measure world population in its simplest form, one simply subtracts deaths from births—or compares crude birth rates (births per 1,000 in the population) to crude death rates (deaths per 1,000). By this metric, the world's population increased very slowly throughout most of human history. For the first 1,000 years of the Common era, the number of people in the world hardly increased at all from a base of about 230 million (Maddison 2006). Some growth occurred over the next 750 years, but the rate of increase was only about 0.1 percent per year. Although women typically bore several children, high death rates erased nearly all this potential growth. About half of newborns died before the age of 5. With the beginning of the industrial revolution and the accompanying improvements in living standards, the world population started on a rapid growth path, rising from about 800 million people in 1750 to about 1 billion in 1800 and then to 2 billion by 1930, 3 billion by 1960, and 5 billion by 1990. Europe and North America experienced the highest growth in the 1800s because of declines in death rates. At the time, both death and birth rates remained high in Asia, Africa, and Latin America (Encyclopedia Britannica 2008).

Beginning in the mid-20th century, improvements in public health, nutrition, sanitation, and other practices developed in economically advanced countries caused a rapid decline in mortality rates in Asia and Latin America. The drop in mortality rates, together with continuing high birth rates, led to sharp increases in population growth. By the 1960s, population growth peaked at about 2 percent per year. In each year, the world's population grew by 68 million. Since then, fertility rates have declined but mortality has been falling as well, lowering the rate of growth but only modestly. Between 1990 and 2005, the world's population increased from 5.26 to 6.44 billion people, a growth rate of about 1.4 percent per year (World Bank 2007). The expansion was and continues to be highest in the lowest income countries, a point we return to later.

Over the next decade, world population growth is expected to decline to 1.1 percent, as birth rates continue to fall.[1] Still, the world population will increase to over 7 billion by 2015. Projections indicate a further slowdown in growth rates, to 1 percent per year from 2015–2025 and to 0.67 percent per year from 2025–2050. The declining growth will ultimately lead to a leveling off of the world's population at nearly 9 billion by mid-century.

The slowing of growth in world population will take place in spite of continuing reductions in infant mortality rates and increases in life expectancy. Between 2005 and 2050, infant deaths per 1,000 live births are expected to drop by over two-thirds, from 46 to 15. Life expectancy at birth is projected to increase by 10 years, from about 65 today to 75 in 2050. The decline in births, from about 20 per 1,000 in 2005 to 14 in 2050, is responsible for all of the reduction in population growth.

Although immigration also plays an important role in population growth for individual countries, natural growth on its own largely explains most population patterns in individual countries. Low-income economies (mainly African and some Asian countries) experienced a higher-than-average 2 percent annual growth between 1990 and 2005, raising their populations by about 600 million people. In contrast, the population of high-income countries increased only 0.7 percent per year, or by about 100 million people (World Bank 2007). Today, nearly 37 percent of the world's population lives in low-income countries, while less than 16 percent reside in high-income countries.

Interestingly, the crude death rate is strikingly similar across the world. Except for sub-Saharan Africa, where there are 17 deaths per 1,000, the typical figure in most of the world is about 9 to 10 per 1,000. But, the crude birth rate is 29 in low-income countries, nearly three times the rate in high-income countries. In sub-Saharan Africa, crude birth rates stood at 40 in 2005. On the other hand, only about 13 births per 1,000 took place in China, a country that accounts for 20 percent of the world's population. India's crude birth rate remains relatively high (at 22 per 1,000 compared to about 10 in high-income countries), but is projected to decline to 13 by 2050, lowering population growth from 1.7 percent today to 0.6 percent in 2050.

Meanwhile, natural population growth in developed economies has already tailed off. In Western Europe, births are approximately equal to deaths, implying zero natural growth. Projections indicate after 2008, deaths in Western Europe will exceed births, leaving immigration as the only source of population growth. But by 2023, even positive immigration flows will not be enough to prevent the population from declining. In Eastern Europe, population decline is already under way, as its total population falls from about 121 million today to 114 million in 2030. Russia's population will fall at an amazingly rapid rate. Between 2008 and 2030, Russia will see its population shrink by over 14 percent, from 141 to 124 million.

Overall, then, the world's population is growing but at slower and more varied rates than in the second half of the 20th century. While birth rates and death rates have continued their downward trajectory, reductions in birth rates are beginning to dominate and ultimately will bring about at most very slow growth in the world's population.

RECENT AND FUTURE POPULATION PATTERNS IN THE UNITED STATES

How do recent and future demographic patterns in the United States compare with this global picture? Our primary interest is how demographic developments are interacting and will interact with the U.S. economy, labor force, educational system, and training. To start, we look at population trends in terms of the nation's changing age distribution, the life cycles of birth cohorts, life expectancy, the morbidity (state of illness or health) of people at various ages, and differences in population patterns by race, ethnic, and socioeconomic status. Although we analyze demographic trends mainly from a U.S. perspective, shifts in less-developed countries are potentially relevant to immigration into the United States.

Current and future population trends are central to government policies at several levels. The negative impacts of the aging of the population are primary concerns in the United States and other developed countries. The worry is that the increasing share of older individuals will create an excessive economic burden on the working-age generation. But population aging is only one of many demographic trends that will influence society. The cycle of enrollments at the elementary, secondary, and post-secondary levels depend mainly on age-specific population trends. Enrollments, in turn, will greatly influence government budgets and class size. Broad population trends will affect the tax base used to fund education, while subgroup trends could influence the need for remedial and other special education services. The adequacy of the labor supply depends not only on the demand for workers in various occupations but the need to replace workers who retire or leave the fields for other occupations.

The demographic trends and patterns in the United States both resemble and depart from trends in most other advanced economies. As of 2008, crude death rates number about 8 per 1,000, a figure only slightly below the rate of 9 in Western Europe. Although life expectancy is higher in other high-income countries, U.S. death rates are lower because of its younger population. American exceptionalism lies in its high crude birth rate of about 14, a rate 40 percent higher than Western Europe. Add in the slightly higher rate of net immigration (about 3 per 1,000 compared with Western Europe's 2 per 1,000) and growth in the U.S. population will average about .9 percent per year when Europe is experiencing zero growth or decline.[2]

In the 20th and early 21st century, the U.S. population doubled from 76 million in 1900 to 151 million in 1950 and doubled again to over 300 million by 2007. The percentage growth in the U.S. population varied by decade but remained above 15 percent (except for the 1930s) until the 1960s (see Figure 2.1). Over the 1970s and 1980s, percentage growth fell to about 11 and 9 percent but rose to 12.4 percent in the 1990s. So far, the rise in the population between 2000 and 2007 period is running at 1 percent per year, or about the pace of the 1970s and 1980s. Natural population growth accounts for most U.S. population growth. But, as we discuss in detail in Chapter 4, net

FIGURE 2.1
Percentage Growth in the U.S. Population by Decade: 1910–2000

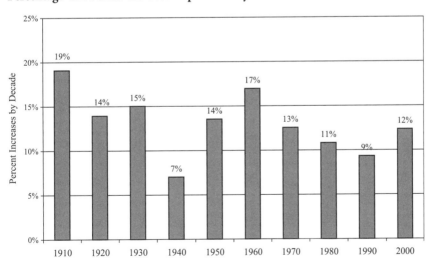

Source: Authors' tabulations of data from U.S. Census Bureau. *Statistical Abstract of the United States:* 2007. Table 1.

immigration (immigrants minus emigrants) began to make up a rising share of population growth beginning in the 1970s, and in the last decade represented over 40 percent of the change in the resident U.S. population (see Figure 2.2).

While crude birth rates less crude death rates equal natural growth, these indicators depend a great deal on the age composition of the population. The behavioral trends in childbearing are best captured by the *total fertility rate*, which measures the number of children women are expected to have in their lifetimes if they follow current age-specific birth rates. In a steady state, the number of births required to replace the current population is about 2.1. Small changes in birth rates can ultimately lead to large changes in the population growth. In the 1920s, women were expected to have about 3 children. The rate fell to about 2.3 in the 1930s, before rising again to a peak of over 3.5 in the late 1950s and early 1960s. Since then, the total fertility rate has declined gradually to about the replacement rate

FIGURE 2.2
Immigrant Share of Population Growth in the Prior Decade, 1920–2006

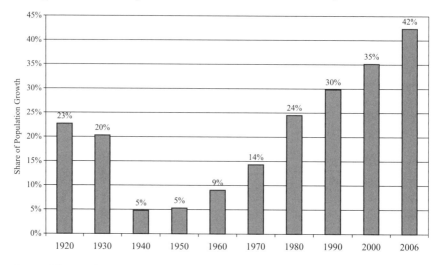

Source: Gibson and Lennon (1999). For 2000 and 2006, tabulated from Statistical Abstract of the United State: 2007, Table 3 and Migration Policy Center Data Hub Table on Number of Foreign-Born by State.

level. The U.S. Census projects total fertility rates will remain low, at 2.06 through 2025 (U.S. Bureau of the Census 2008).

Death rates that take account of the age distribution (age-adjusted death rates) declined at a surprisingly similar rate in the first and last halves of the 20th century. In both the 1900–1950 and 1950–2000 periods, the age-adjusted death rate fell by about 45 percent for men; the declines among women were even more rapid, with death rates falling by 67 and 52 percent.[3] If current death rates by age were similar to those that prevailed in 1900, about 26 of every 1,000 people would die each year instead of about 10 in 2000.

Another way to think about death rates is to focus on premature deaths. The common demographic indicator is the number of years resulting from various causes of death in a specific year. If 10 of every 1,000 people died before age 75 at an average age of 64, the years lost to premature death would be 110 (11 years times 10 deaths). Between 1980 and 2004, the number of years lost to premature death declined from about 10.4 to 7.3 per 100 people. This 36 percent reduction was higher than the decline in death rates, indicating that reductions in mortality were even more important for the under 75 population than for those ages 75 and older.

Upward trends in life expectancy mirror the decline in premature years lost. Over the last 25 years, the expected years of remaining life rose substantially. Life expectancy at birth increased from 73.7 to almost 77.7 years, while life expectancy at age 65 rose by over two years, from 16.5 in 1980 to 18.7 in 2004. While high, these figures are actually below the life expectancy levels in many other advanced economies. In Canada, France, Italy, and Sweden, life expectancy at birth has reached 80 or slightly higher. Although determining the precise reasons for the differences is difficult (Deaton and Paxton 2001), improving the efficiency of the U.S. health system and reducing the impact of life-style and other external factors are more likely to close the gap than added spending (Joumard et al. 2008).

Measuring the health of the U.S. population involves a number of indicators. One is the share of individuals who experience a limitation of activity, defined as a long-term reduction in a person's capacity to perform usual activities associated with their age group due to at least one chronic condition. About 12 percent of the U.S. population faces such a limitation. Not surprisingly, limitations are sharply higher among older populations. Between 1998–2000 and 2004–2006, the elderly experienced a modest decline in a long-term limitation, with the rate falling from 36.6 percent to 33.6 percent for the 65 and over population. Another indicator is self-reported health status. On this indicator, the health of the population has improved substantially since the early 1980s. The share of people rating their health as fair or poor declined for all age groups, especially older individuals. In 1982, over 21 percent of 45- to 64-year-olds and 35 percent of those 65 and over rated their health as fair or poor. By 2006, the proportions had fallen to 15 and 26 percent.

The joint gains in welfare from improved health and added life expectancy have been enormous. One attempt to place a monetary value on the gains in the United States between 1970 and 2000 yields the extraordinary figure of $3.2 trillion per year, or nearly half the average GDP in these decades (Murphy and Topel 2005). The estimates indicate that health outlays offset about 36 percent of the gross social value of $95 trillion.

Notwithstanding these improvements in self-reported health, healthy life expectancy (life expectancy at birth minus years of ill health) is lower in the United States than in other advanced economies, according to the World Health Organization.[4] The United States falls short in terms of healthy life expectancy by about 3 years relative to Australia, Canada, France, Germany, and Italy (69.3 years in the United States compared to nearly 72 in the other countries).

For the next several decades, the U.S. population will grow because of natural population growth and immigration.[5] Death rates are projected to increase from 8.3 per 1,000 in 2008 to 8.9 in 2030 and 9.7 in 2050, as the aging of the population offsets rising age-specific life expectancy. But, birth rates will continue to exceed death rates. Although the number of births per 1,000 is projected to fall slightly from 14.2 in 2008 to about 13 in 2040 and through 2050, these levels and the projected death rates are expected to generate modest levels of natural population growth, about 0.45 percent per year. Without immigration, the U.S. population would grow by about 19 percent from 2008 to 2050. Such growth would be less than half of the total population growth the United States has experienced in recent decades. With immigration, total population growth is projected to reach 0.87 percent per year. This rate is well below what the United States experienced in recent decades. Still, with the U.S. population in 2050 projected to reach 439 million people, the United States will be accommodating over one-third more people in 2050 than in 2008.

THE CHANGING COMPOSITION OF THE U.S. POPULATION

The age composition of a country both causes and is affected by future population growth. Population projections begin with an initial age composition, say as of 2000. If we ignore immigration for the moment, the projected number of 15- to 19-year-olds in 2010 is equal to the number of 5- to 9-year-olds in 2000 that survive for the subsequent 10 years. Then, once we apply age-specific survival rates to each age group, we obtain a projection for the number in the population 10 or 20 years later who are 10 or 20 years older. Age-specific birth rates times the number of women at specific childbearing ages determine the number of births in any year; adjusted for survival rates, the newborns in year 1 become 10-year-olds 10 years later.

Given an initial age distribution, a proportional reduction in death rates for each age group will leave the age distribution constant. The impact of age-specific birth rates is more complex. A decline in age-specific birth rates will lower the number of births in the short run and will lead to a subsequent decline starting 15 to 20 years later because of the decline in the number of women in childbearing years. To reverse the initial decline in births requires large increases in age-specific birth rates that are enough to offset the smaller number of women in childbearing years. The standard projections suggest no such reversal for high-income countries, including the United States, Japan, and Western Europe.

Instead, the population will become older and have fewer people in the 25- to 54-year-old age group. The U.S. age pattern over time runs in the same direction as trends in Western Europe and Japan but at a much slower pace. Note in Figure 2.3 the proportion of 25- to 54-year-olds drops almost as rapidly in the United States as in Western Europe, although far less than in Japan. The magnitude of increases in the over 65 share of the U.S. population (from 12.5 to about 20 percent) is dwarfed by the much larger increases in the elderly in Western Europe and Japan (Figure 2.4). If current projections materialize, 37 percent of Japan's population and 29 percent of Western Europe's population will be over 65 in 2050.

FIGURE 2.3
Share of Population Age 25–54 in the U.S., Western European, and Japan: 2000–2050

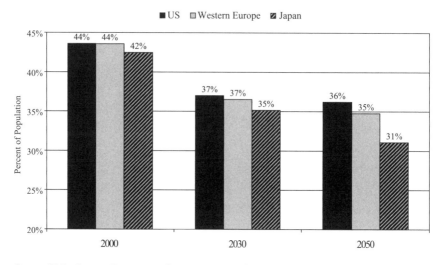

Source: U.S. Census Bureau, on-line International Data Base, http://www.census.gov/ipc/www/idb/.

FIGURE 2.4
Share of Population Age 65 and Over in the U.S., Western Europe, and Japan: 2000–2050

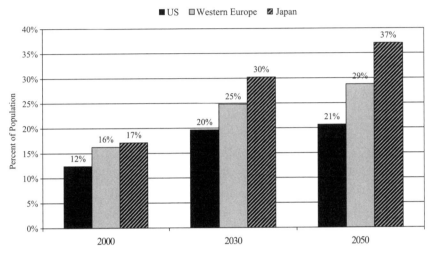

Source: See Figure 2.3.

The reasons for aging differ somewhat between the United States and most other advanced economies. Older people are living longer in all advanced countries. The United States is exceptional in sustaining a replacement level of fertility, while fertility in Europe and Japan is falling far short of levels required to replace the current population. A good example of the importance of fertility is its role in the dramatic aging of South Korea. The total fertility rate was only 1.2 births per South Korean woman and is projected to rise only to about 1.4, far below the 2.1 replacement level the United States is maintaining. As a result, Korea's 65 and over population is expected to jump 7 percent of the population in 2000, to 22 percent by 2030, and to nearly 33 percent by 2050.

The birth dearth is striking in Europe. In the European Union as a whole, completed fertility per woman already 40 or older is 1.72 and is projected to fall to 1.54, rates below the 2.07 to 2.10 levels required for replacement. However, several countries, notably France, Ireland, and Norway, have total fertility rates

1.9 or higher. Countries with rates above 1.8 include Denmark, the Netherlands, the United Kingdom, and Sweden. At the low end, with 1.4 or fewer births expected per woman, are Austria, Belgium, Germany, Italy, Spain, and Poland.

RISING DIVERSITY IN THE UNITED STATES

With a population almost two-thirds the size of the enlarged European Union, the United States can be thought of as more like a continent than an individual country. So, just as we see population patterns vary among countries within Europe, we expect variations within the United States. The geographic patterns of the growth and composition of the U.S. population are complicated by internal and external immigration, topics we cover in later chapters. In this section, we take a look at population patterns across variables measured for the nation as a whole, including race and ethnic origin.

Considering the common racial classifications of white, black, Asian, and others (including mixed race individuals), as well as Hispanic/non-Hispanic ethnicity (of any race), we see rapid increases in diversity and declines in the share of the population that is white and non-Hispanic. From 2000 to 2050, the proportion classified as white, non-Hispanic is projected to fall from nearly 70 percent to 50 percent of the U.S. population. The main but not the only reason is a near tripling of the number of Hispanic individuals from 35 million in 2000 to 102 million in 2050. As a result, the Hispanic proportion of the U.S. population will nearly double from 12.6 to 24.4 percent. Asian Americans will also double their share of the U.S. population, from 4 to 8 percent. Black Americans will experience a more modest gain of 2 percentage points, from 12.6 to 14.7 percent of the population.

IMPLICATIONS FOR THE WORKFORCE

Two questions dominate concerns about the job market implications of demographic trends: (1) will we have a large enough workforce to pay for the health and retirement benefits of the expanding older population? and (2) will the slowing growth of the workforce lead to labor market shortages and thereby weaken the U.S. economy?

The patterns by age and sex are a good place to start. The population of 25- to 59-year-olds usually contributes most to the workforce, to incomes, and to productivity. Moreover, this middle-age period is the only time in the life cycle when what we produce is greater than what we consume, either from public or private sources (Lee 2007). When people are young, they earn little while consuming out of their parents' incomes and using up public resources primarily in the educational system. Beginning in their early 60s, earnings begin to fall to the level of their total consumption, which in turn is financed privately or through government benefits. Only in their prime age years do people earn enough to transfer resources to other groups. If the pool of 25- to 59-year-olds making the transfers declines as a share of the overall population, then either people in young or old age groups must accept less, or prime-age workers must contribute a higher share of their incomes. Between 2008 and 2030, the 25- to 59-year-old will decline from about 48 to 42 percent of the population. Thus, the age group that earns more resources than it consumes will be declining over the next few decades.

Overall, the growth in the workforce will be slowing over the coming decades relative to population growth. Between 1977 and 2007, the size of the workforce increased by 1.45 percent per year, while the population grew only 1 percent per year. The share of the population in the active workforce rose from 45 percent in 1997 to 51 percent in 2007. The reversal expected between 2010 and 2030 is striking. Although annual growth in the population will slow modestly from about 1 to 0.8, the expansion of the workforce will drop much more, assuming men and women in each age group have the same tendency to work as they do today. Labor force growth amounted to 1.4 percent per year between 1977 and 2007 but will decline to only 0.5 per year from 2010 until 2030 (Toosi 2006). The active workforce will fall back to 47 percent of the population in 2030.

The main reason for the slowdown is demographic—the share of the population in their prime working years is declining. Another reason is that the rise in women's workforce activity over the last several decades has played itself out and is no longer a source of future growth in the workforce. Through the 1960s, 1970s, and 1980s, the rate at which women (ages 16 and over) participated in the workforce rose rapidly, from about 38 percent to 57 by 1990. Since then, women's labor force participation rate has moved up very slowly and may have peaked at about 60 percent.[6]

Growth in the workforce will increasingly be concentrated on older workers. From 2010 to 2020, the number of 25- to 54-year-old workers will rise by only 1.5 percent, compared with a projected 23 percent increase for workers, ages 55 to 64, and a 68 percent increase for workers 65 and over. Projections indicate that workers 55 and over will account for all of approximately 10 million worker increase between 2010 and 2020. The number of 16- to 24-year-old and 45- to 54-year-old workers will decline by about 4.5 million, offset by an increase in 25- to 44-year-olds.

One uncertainty about future labor force growth is the extent to which older individuals (65 and older) will choose to stay in the workforce. Currently, of the 65 and older population, about 13 percent of women and 21 percent of men are in the labor force. But, after decades of declining workforce participation for older people, the trends have moved in a positive direction since the late 1990s. In 1999, when the unemployment rate was at its low point and jobs were abundant, 17 percent of older men and 9 percent of older women participated in the workforce. By mid-2008, workforce participation rates had risen four percentage points to 21 percent for men and 13 percent for women. If these increases continued for the 65 and over population, so that 20 percent of women and 30 percent of men were in the labor force, then the 2030 workforce would be 12.7 percent larger than in 2008, instead of the current projection of 9.3 percent growth based on an assumption of constant labor force participation rates.[7]

Improving health for the older population is one of several reasons for expecting increases in their labor force participation to continue. Since the early 1980s, the percentage of 65- to 74-year-olds describing their health as fair or poor has declined from 34 to 22 percent (Johnson 2007). Employment rates are substantially higher for the 55 and over population reporting very good health than good or fair health. Other factors causing people to continue working past age 65 are that jobs are becoming less physically demanding, Social Security's retirement age is increasing, private pensions are becoming less adequate with the shift from defined benefit to defined contribution systems (Munnell and Sass 2007), Social Security's financial disincentives to keep working have been eliminated (Song 2004), and life expectancy is rising faster for workers with above average earnings (Waldron 2007). While the financial incentives for staying in the workforce vary with age, income, and type of pension (Butrica, Johnson, Smith, and Steuerle 2006), on average each added year of work increases a worker's income in retirement by an average of 9 percent (Johnson 2007).

Since older workers are less likely to work full-time than prime-age workers, the number of older workers in the labor force overstates their contribution. Prime-age workers, ages 25 to 54, average about 33 percent more hours per year in jobs than workers 65 and over and about 4 percent more than 55- to 64-year-olds workers. Thus, although 25- to 54-year-olds will make up about 63 percent of workers in 2020, they will account for about 69 percent of hours worked.[8]

How will declining growth in the workforce affect economic growth? According to the Vice Chairman of the Federal Reserve Board (Kohn 2007), the aging of the workforce will lower the long-term growth rate in GDP from about 3.2 percent to about 2.2 percent, even assuming healthy increases in productivity (output per worker). Still, it is possible that increased labor productivity will offset some of the impact of low labor force growth. Productivity depends in part on the amount of capital per worker. If the growth in new equipment, which often embodies new technologies, remains at past levels and labor force growth declines, then growth in capital per worker will increase, potentially raising productivity growth.

Demography's impact on the composition of the workforce, however, might limit productivity gains. In addition to the aging of the workforce, dramatic changes by race and Hispanic status of the prime age workforce will be taking place. As Figure 2.5 reveals, the population of non-Hispanic whites in this age group will be about 12 million lower in 2030 and 2050 than in 2000. At the same time, the Hispanic population in this age group is projected to rise by about 12 million through 2030 and by 23 million by 2050. Growth in this prime age population will be quite rapid for Asians as well. By 2050, there will be 10 million more Asian-Americans at ages 25 to

FIGURE 2.5
Change in 25–54 Year-Old Population by Race and Ethnicity: 2000–2050

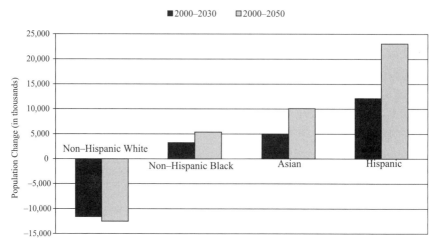

Source: Tabulated from U.S. Bureau of the Census, tables from U.S. Interim Projections by Age, Sex, Race, and Hispanic Origin: 2000–2050. http://www.census.gov/population/www/projections/usinterimproj/.

54 than in 2000. The non-Hispanic black population will rise, but at a much smaller pace than among Hispanics and Asians. Taken together, these changes will likely require enhanced efforts to achieve effective teamwork and communication among an increasingly diverse workforce.

Demographic patterns have implications for specific education and occupation levels of the coming workforce. In recent years, we have witnessed a striking upgrading in the educational composition of the labor force, especially if we consider net additional workers. Between 1992 and early 2007, the adult labor force (ages 25 and over) expanded by about 24 million workers. Over the same period, workers with a BA increased by 15.5 million, and workers with at least some college rose by an additional 7.9 million. Additional workers with no college amounted to only about 400,000, or 2 percent of the overall net changes. This number looks implausible given that over 40 percent of a recent cohort of 25- to 29-year-olds had no more than a high school diploma.[9] Two phenomena help explain the seemingly divergent pattern. First, the inflow of less-educated young people and immigrants into the labor force was offset by an outflow of less-educated older workers. Second, labor force participation rates are lower among less-educated than among more-educated workers.

In the coming years, the replacement of older workers with more-educated younger cohorts will not lead to similar gains because the current workforce nearing retirement is more highly educated than past retirees and has an educational distribution similar to workers who recently entered the job market. Compare first the education levels of the group leaving the workforce in the recent past (people over 64) with the recently entering the full-time job market (25- to 34-year-olds). One in four people over age 64 did not complete high school, while only 13 percent of 25- to 34-year-olds lacked a high school degree. Only 19 percent of the 65 and older cohort completed a BA degree compared to 31 percent of 25- to 34-year-olds.[10] In contrast, today's 55- to 64-year-olds have nearly the same educational attainment as 25- to 34-year-olds—13 percent attained less than a high school diploma and 30 percent graduated college. Thus, over the next ten years, we are unlikely to see a substantial net gain in education as young entrants replace the retiring cohort. In fact, the lower than average educational attainment among minorities, combined with their increased share of the workforce, could mean declining or stagnant educational levels for the workforce, with new entrants having less education than new retirees.

Demography will influence the availability of occupational skills as well. Although the data on occupational skills are less easy to aggregate, many skilled occupations will experience large outflows of workers because of aging and retirement. As a result, employers will have to replace skilled workers in many occupations. Nearly half (45 percent) will be jobs requiring some postsecondary training but not a BA degree. For example, employment in five skilled construction trades is expected to grow by 10 to 15 percent and provide 4.6 million job openings, while jobs in installation, maintenance, repair, and transportation will grow at similar rates and together generate more than 4 million additional openings (Holzer and Lerman 2007).

The result of population aging and other demographic trends may not cause a labor shortage, as long as immigration increases or production is shifted offshore (Freeman 2007). However, at expected immigration rates and with no major shifts in educational outcomes of labor force subgroups, employers and some workers will face significant challenges. Employers will have to adjust by learning more about recruiting and retaining older workers, using limited term contracts to bring back former employees, making hours more flexible, and reshaping pension compensation (Robson 2001). One potentially positive pattern for employers is the higher ratio of older, experienced workers who can train and mentor young workers. At the same time, the traditional pyramid structure will become a more uniform age distribution. The result may be to frustrate newer or younger workers, who will have fewer chances to move up in their company, as the same leaders will remain in top positions for longer. To get around this potential problem, Robson (2001) suggests assigning older workers to special projects, thereby creating more openings at the top. Other approaches are to compensate workers more on the basis of competencies than on the worker's title and to make greater use of teams with older workers as mentors.

The increase in older workers that comes along with the aging of the baby boom is likely to slow wage growth for this group. Older workers are not pure substitutes for younger workers (Triest, Sass, and Sapozhnikov 2006). As a result, the added crowding at older ages is likely to lower wages, potentially lowering the growth in the labor supply of older workers.

Finally, population aging and the associated labor force implications are key drivers of the rapid growth in government spending on Old Age, Survivors, and Disability Insurance (Social Security), Medicare, and Medicaid.[11] Although the challenges from population aging in the United States are modest compared to the problems of financing older individuals in other advanced countries (Organisation for Economic Cooperation and Development [OECD] 2006), the changing U.S. age distribution will place rising burdens on a slowly growing workforce. The number of U.S. workers per Social Security recipient will decline from 3.2 in 2008 to 2.1 in 2030 (Congressional Budget Office [CBO] 2007).

The potential rise in the payroll tax burden required to pay the added expense of these programs because of population aging might well result in distortions that reduce economic growth. According to the CBO (2007), aging will be the main reason for the rising costs of Social Security (Old Age Insurance) and contribute to rising government spending on health care. Under current laws, spending on Social Security, Medicaid, and Medicare will jump from about 8.3 percent of GDP to over 15 percent of GDP by 2035. Demography plays a large role in the rising costs. Spending on these three programs would be nearly 40 percent lower if population aging was not a factor (CBO 2007). Rising health costs accounts for most of the remaining increases. Since the Social Security tax constitutes only 6 percent of GNP and the income tax only about 8 percent of GDP, the payroll tax, income tax, and/or deficit required to fund these programs would have to rise by about 50 percent to pay for the added costs of these entitlement programs.[12] The increased tax rates might reduce the supply of labor and thereby worsen the decline in labor force growth and GDP growth.

Unless the United States changes the law, demography and rising health costs will generate sharp increases in taxes and/or government budget deficits (CBO 2007). Some countries, including Sweden, have attempted to limit these increased burdens by indexing the age at full retirement to increases in life expectancy: each added year of life expectancy raises the age at which people become eligible for full retirement benefits. In the United States, without any adjustment for increased life expectancy, about 20 percent of the U.S. population will be eligible for Medicare and full Social Security benefits in 2050 (Shoven and Godi 2008), up from 12 percent today. Even if the government began a life expectancy adjustment in 2004, the share eligible for benefits would jump from 12 to 17 percent of the population.

IMPLICATIONS FOR EDUCATION

For elementary and secondary education, the aging of the U.S. population brings with it concerns over school finance. Poterba (1997, 1998) and Hoxby (1998) report that per-capita education spending decreases as the proportion of the population over age 65 increases, due to the propensity of older voters to vote against education finance measures. Poterba (1998) estimates that the projected rise in the share of older residents in the United States from 12.5 to 20 percent in the coming years (as reported earlier), will result in a roughly 12 percent decrease in per-pupil education spending. Compared to the current average per-pupil spending of $10,788, this translates to a sizable $1,294 less per student.

These results make sense if older voters are motivated by pure self-interest. With their own children out of school, older residents have little reason to vote for education spending and may prefer spending on other public goods from which they receive more direct benefits, reflecting tensions between generations in the allocation of public funds (Poterba 1997). On the other hand, one might argue that older voters gain some benefits from the "spillovers" of a more-educated population. They may experience reductions in crime or gain from the increased productivity of the local workforce, but the empirical evidence on the voting patterns of older Americans suggests that the former point dominates.

Adding to these apparent intergenerational tensions, Poterba (1997) found that the negative correlation between age and education spending becomes even more pronounced when older and younger cohorts are predominantly from different racial backgrounds. As younger cohorts of the U.S. population become increasingly more diverse, it is likely that education spending will continue to decrease, although it is possible that this effect will be mitigated if older generations adopt different attitudes toward race in the years to come.

Other shifts in the attitudes of older voters are also possible. Interestingly, there is evidence that older voters actually encouraged education spending in the early 20th century. Goldin and Katz (1997) found that the share of older voters was actually positively correlated with the growth of high schools in the 1920s, and Hoxby (1998) found a similar positive relationship in 1900 and 1910. Over the intervening decades, however, Hoxby (1998) found that the relationship became negative and confirms Poterba's (1997) findings with statistically significant negative results in the 1990s. What accounts for the change? One hypothesis is that older voters had stronger ties to their community in the early 20th century. If their children and grandchildren lived nearby, these voters may have been more likely to support local schools.

Another concern about the adequacy of school finance comes from projected changes in cohort size. As shown in Figure 2.6, the population of school-age children dipped in the 1980s, but increased substantially in the 1990s. Over the course of the 1990s, the population of children age 5 to 17 expanded 17 percent overall, translating to a 1.7 percent average annual increase. Most of this increase is attributed to increased immigration and higher fertility rates (Hussar and Bailey 2007). Since attendance rates in U.S. elementary schools are high, enrollments closely mirror this increase.

Although population and enrollment growth slowed somewhat in the last five years, the U.S. Department of Education projects that elementary and secondary school enrollments will continue their uphill climb in the coming years, although the rate of increase will be substantially lower than in the 1990s. Between 2006 and 2016, enrollments are likely to increase by 7.6 percent overall, resulting in an additional 4.3 million

FIGURE 2.6
Expenditures on Education and Actual and Projected Enrollment: 1970–2016

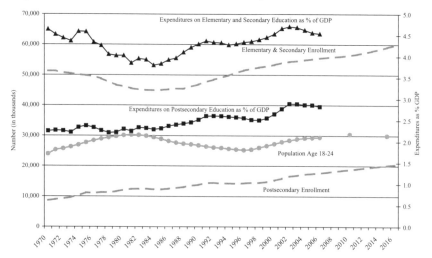

Source: U.S. Department of Education, Digest of Education Statistics (2007) and Census Bureau, U.S. Statistical Abstract (2008).

students in U.S. elementary and secondary schools (author's tabulations on U.S. Department of Education 2007 data).

What is the connection between cohort size and education spending? The connection is more tenuous than one might imagine. Expenditures per student in elementary and secondary schools more than doubled in real terms over the past several decades, from roughly $4,832 in 1970 to $10,788 in 2006. However, as a percentage of U.S. GDP, education spending on kindergarten through 12th grade was about the same in 1970 as in 2006 (top line in Figure 2.6). The expenditure share did increase in the 1990s (to a high of 4.7 percent in 2001), but only after a decrease in the 1980s (to a low of 3.8 percent in 1984). Note that expenditures show more variability and slightly different timing than enrollment increases. Spending as a share of GDP stagnated in the early 1990s when enrollment was rising rapidly, suggesting that the number of students may not be the primary determinant of school spending.

Literature in the economics of education confirms this point. Poterba (1997) analyzed changes in spending within states over time and found that larger school-age cohorts received fewer resources on a per-student basis than smaller cohorts. If current policies and practices continue, then future students—particularly those in states and localities with larger school-age populations—may find themselves facing even tighter budgets in the future.

How do these patterns compare to other developed countries? The United States spends somewhat more on elementary and secondary education as a percentage of GDP (4.5 percent) than the OECD average of 3.8 percent (OECD 2007, Table B2.2, p. 206). But, spending does not necessarily translate into high performance. Norway, a country in which students perform at the top on international tests, spends 4.6 percent of its GDP on K-12 education and roughly $1,000 more per student. But Japanese students also perform well relative to U.S. students on almost all measures (U.S. Department of Education 2006, Table 397), yet Japan spends only 2.7 percent of its

GDP on its primary and secondary education and almost $4,000 less per student (U.S. Department of Education 2006, Table 412 and 413).[13]

Adding postsecondary education spending to elementary and secondary shows the United States outspending other OECD nations by a considerable margin, over 7 percent of GDP compared with an OECD average of 5.7 percent (see Figure 2.7). In terms of dollars per student, the United States spends about 50 percent more than the OECD average. As of 2004, the U.S. figure was over $12,000 per pupil. Switzerland and Norway come closest in annual expenditures, at $11,800 and $10,700, respectively. France and Germany averaged less than $8,000 per student. Although the United States pays considerably more per student at all levels of education than other large, advanced countries, the biggest gaps are in postsecondary education. As a nation, we spend $373 billion or 2.8 percent of GDP (U.S. Department of Education 2007) on colleges,

FIGURE 2.7
Elementary, Secondary, and Postsecondary Education Spending as Percent of GDP

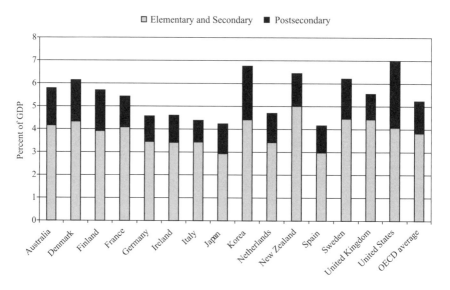

Source: OECD, Education at a Glance (2007), Table B2.1.

universities, and other postsecondary training. In 2004, outlays per college student were over $22,000 in the United States, about double the per student figures for France, Germany, Japan, and the United Kingdom (OECD 2007, Table B1.1a).

Future spending on U.S. postsecondary education is likely to rise rapidly because of increasing enrollments in elementary and secondary education and the increasing value of a college education. Returning to Figure 2.6, we see steady increases in postsecondary enrollments over the entire period from 1970 to 2006, despite a decrease in the population age 18 to 24 in the 1980s and 1990s. Much of this increase in college-going was undoubtedly driven by increasing wage returns to a college education over this period. As our economy continues to move away from manufacturing and toward service and information-based industries, the returns to a college education will remain high. As a result, continued, though slightly slower, increases in postsecondary enrollment are likely over the coming decade,

FIGURE 2.8
Postsecondary Enrollment by Age: 1970–2016

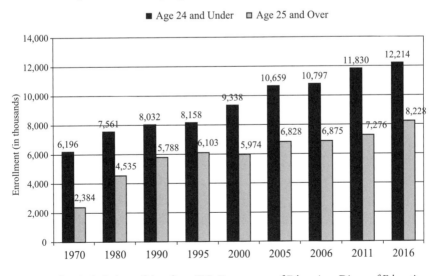

Source: Authors' tabulations of data from U.S. Department of Education, *Digest of Education Statistics* (2007), Table 181.

even though the population in the 18 to 24 age group will remain constant.

Interestingly, projections of enrollment increases do not appear to be getting through to the colleges themselves. A recent article in the *Washington Post* (Strauss 2008) highlighted the fear among institutions of higher education of a leveling-off in college-going. In the article, college presidents expressed concern over increased competition for students—a problem that will likely end up benefitting potential students. Much of this fear is fuelled by a report of the Western Interstate Commission for Higher Education (WICHE) of a dip in the number of traditional high school graduates. Although its methodology is unclear, WICHE's projections made headlines by suggesting that that the number of high school graduates would begin its decline as early as 2008. What was less widely reported is that the expected decline is only moderate (by 150,000 students nationwide at most), and that this number is expected to more than recover by 2020 (authors' tabulations of data from WICHE, Table 2.2, p. 6).

The focus on the college-age population fails to capture the astounding increase in college-going among older, nontraditional students. These students undoubtedly account for the difference between the population projections and postsecondary enrollment trends depicted in Figure 2.6—and they will likely sustain demand for an education college. In fact, since 1970 the number of nontraditional college students, age 25 and over, has almost tripled—from just over 2.3 million to 6.8 million, as shown in Figure 2.8. As the population ages, we can expect more nontraditional students to enroll in college—more than 8 million are projected to enroll by 2016 (U.S. Department of Education 2007).

The increase in nontraditional student enrollment will also cause substantial shifts in the demand for certain types of college degree programs. For example, nontraditional students are overrepresented in public community colleges: nationwide, students age 25 and over represent 42 percent of all enrollments in community colleges, compared to just 31 percent in public four-year institutions (U.S. Department of Education 2007, Table 183). In states with strong community college systems, the proportion is even higher—in California nontraditional students account for 53 percent of enrollments (Cellini 2005).

The popularity of community colleges among nontraditional students likely derives from their low tuition, flexible scheduling, and short-term vocationally-oriented degree and certificate programs (Cellini 2005). Part-time programs are likely to become even more popular in all types of postsecondary institutions in the coming years as nontraditional students are more likely to attend school while working. A weakening economy will further increase this demand as workers try to hold on to jobs while upgrading their skills. On the other hand, rising unemployment may increase demand for full-time coursework as laid-off workers seek training for new careers.

What is unmistakable in the face of economic change, however, is that the demand for workplace-relevant education and training will rise. While our public community colleges can meet some of this demand with their vocational coursework, we should also expect a rise in private-sector education and training, as for-profit colleges (also known as career colleges, proprietary schools, or technical institutes) have been shown to compete with public community colleges and may respond more quickly than public institutions to changes in demand for new skills (Cellini 2007).

CONCLUSIONS

Population aging and declining rates of population growth are positive developments for the world in general and the United States in particular. Rising life expectancy and healthy aging are enormously valuable to people. According to one estimate, the cumulative gains in health and life expectancy during the 20th century were worth over $1.2 million per person for men and women (Murphy and Topel 2005). As noted above, the increased longevity between 1970 and 2000 is estimated to have generated about $3.2 trillion per year to national wealth. Health expenses offset less than 40 percent of these benefits. Declining birth rates in the less-developed world offer considerable hope that expansions in national income will translate into rising living standards.

With increased life expectancy and slowing birth rates will come changes in the age distribution of the population. In particular, prime-age workers—people in the age groups that produce more than they consume—will make up a declining share of the population, while the resources required from this group will rise sharply. By 2030, the number of workers per social security recipient will fall to 2.1. The workforce will face a substantially expanded burden to pay for retirement income and health benefits for the rising number of people 62 and over.

Population aging will slow the growth in the workforce, alter the profile of workers, and change the wage distribution. One way to mitigate the implied rise in government spending and tax rates is to do more to encourage older workers to stay in the job market. Despite their improved health and jobs that are less physically demanding, older workers have been retiring much earlier than in prior decades. A substantial share of the impact on tax burdens associated with population aging could be offset by an increase in labor force participation by the 55 and over population (Johnson, Mermin, and Steuerle 2006).

The aging of the U.S. population will influence labor markets and education as well. Employers will become more reliant on older workers as the share of prime-age workers declines. The scarcity of younger workers will encourage firms to improve training, mentoring, and teamwork, as prime-age and older workers are paired with fewer people at the beginning of their careers. Support for added education spending might slow because of the increased burden of supporting the older population and the declining support from older voters. On the other hand, people may realize that the scarcity of young workers and the increased burden of social insurance programs will make the education and training of the future workforce a priority.

Aging is only one of the major demographic changes that is changing society, the job market, and education. We next turn to the role of major shifts in the population associated with family structure, immigration, and internal migration.

NOTES

1. All figures in the next four paragraphs come from the International Data Base, prepared by the International Activities Center, U.S. Bureau of the Census. The main page for the IDB is http://www.census.gov/ipc/www/idb/index.html. Similar figures are available from the Department of Economic and Social Affairs, Population Division, UN, http://www.un.org/esa/population/unpop.htm.

2. See footnote 1 for the source of the International Data Base figures.

3. The data cited in this and subsequent paragraphs on mortality and morbidity come from National Center for Health Statistics (2007).

4. See tables on Healthy Life Expectancy at birth, http://www.who.int/whosis/en/index.html.

5. Figures in this paragraph involve calculations by the authors from the International Data Base. See footnote 1.

6. The figures in this and subsequent two paragraphs come from tabulations by the authors from data extracted from the U.S. Bureau of Labor Statistics Web site, www.bls.gov.

7. Projections by the Bureau of Labor Statistics are for the labor force participation rates of the 65 and older population to rise to 25 percent of men and 17 percent of women (Toosi 2006).

8. Authors' calculation using microdata from the 2007 Current Population Survey.

9. These numbers were tabulated by the author from the U.S. Bureau of Labor Statistics Web site.

10. These data come from author's tabulations of the March 2007 Current Population Survey.

11. Other major factors are that health expenditures per person are rising faster than GDP and that social security pensions have formulas that generate faster growth than GDP.

12. The data come from the Council of Economic Advisers (2007). A rise from 14.3 percent to 21 percent of GDP implies about a 50 percent increases in taxes.

13. Per-student calculations are the sum of the differences in elementary and secondary between the United States and the other country from National Center for Education Statistics 2006, Table 412.

REFERENCES

Butrica, Barbara, Richard Johnson, Karen Smith, and C. Eugene Steuerle. 2006. "The Implicit Tax on Work at Older Ages." *National Tax Journal* June: 211–34.

Cellini, Stephanie Riegg. 2005. "Community Colleges and Proprietary Schools: A Comparison of Sub-Baccalaureate Institutions." California Center for Population Research (CCPR) Working Paper No. 012-05. University of California, Los Angeles.

Cellini, Stephanie Riegg. Forthcoming. "Crowded Colleges and College Crowd-Out: The Impact of Public Subsidies on the Two-Year College Market." *American Economic Journal: Economic Policy.*

Congressional Budget Office. 2007. *The Long-term Budget Outlook.* Congress of the United States. http://www.cbo.gov/ftpdocs/88xx/doc8877/12-13-LTBO.pdf.

Deaton, Angus, and Christina Paxton. 2001. "Mortality, Income, and Income Inequality over Time." Working Paper 8534. Cambridge, MA: National Bureau of Economic Research.

Eberstadt, Nicholas, and Hans Groth. 2007. *Europe's Coming Demographic Challenge: Unlocking the Value of Health.* Washington, DC: American Enterprise Institute.

Ehrlich, Paul. 1968. *The Population Bomb.* New York: Ballantine Books.

Encyclopedia Britannica Online. 2008. "Population." Accessed August 3, 2008.

Freeman, Richard. 2007. "Is a Great Labor Shortage Coming? Replacement Demand in the Global Economy." In *Reshaping the American Workforce in a Changing Economy,* ed. Harry J. Holzer and Demetra Smith Nightingale. Washington, DC: Urban Institute Press.

Gibson, Campbell J., and Emily Lennon. 1999. "Historical Census Statistics on the Foreign-born Population of the United States, 1850–1990." Population Division Working Paper No. 29. Washington, DC: U.S. Bureau of the Census.

Goldin, Claudia, and Lawrence Katz. 1997. "Why the United States Led in Education: Lessons from Secondary School Expansion, 1910–1940." National Bureau of Economic Research Working Paper No. 6144.

Holzer, Harry, and Robert Lerman. 2007. *America's Forgotten Middle-Skill Jobs.* Washington, DC: Workforce Alliance.

Hoxby, Caroline M. 1998. "How Much Does School Spending Depend on Family Income? The Historical Origins of the Current School Finance Dilemma." *American Economic Review* 88(2): 309–14.

Hussar, William J., and Tabitha M. Bailey. 2007. *Projections of Education Statistics to 2016.* Washington, DC: U.S. Department of Education.

Johnson, Richard. 2007. "Should People Work Longer, and Will They?" Washington, DC: Urban Institute Press. http://www.urban.org/publications/411584.html.

Johnson, Richard, Gordon Mermin, and Eugene Steuerle. 2006. *Work Impediments at Older Ages.* The Retirement Project Discussion Paper 06-02. Washington, DC: Urban Institute Press.

Joumard, Isabelle, Christophe André, Chantal Nicq, and Olivier Chatal. 2008. "Health Status Determinants: Lifestyle, Environment, Health Care Resources, and Efficiency." OECD Economics Department Working Paper No. 627. Paris: OECD Publishing.

Kohn, Donald. 2007. "The aging workforce." Testimony before the Special Committee on Aging, U.S. Senate. http://www.federalreserve.gov/newsevents/testimony/Kohn20070228a.htm#fs6.

Lee, Ronald. 2007. *Global Population and Its Economic Consequences.* Washington, DC: American Enterprise Institute.

Maddison, Angus. 2006. *The World Economy: A Millennial Perspective.* Paris: Organization for Economic Cooperation and Development.

Meadows, Donella, Dennis Meadows, et al. 1972. *The Limits to Growth: A Report for the Club of Rome's Project on the Predicament of Mankind.* New York: New American Library.

Munnell, Alicia, and Steven A. Sass. 2007. "The Labor Supply of Older Americans." Working Paper No. 6. Boston: Center for Retirement Research, Boston College. http://crr.bc.edu/working_papers/the_labor_supply_of_older_americans.html.

Murphy, Kevin, and Robert Topel. 2005. "The Value of Health and Longevity." Working Paper 11405. Cambridge, MA: National Bureau of Economic Research.

National Center for Health Statistics. 2007. *Health, 2007, With Chartbook on Trends in the Health of Americans.* Hyattsville, MD: National Center for Health Statistics.

Organisation for Economic Cooperation and Development. 2006. *Live Longer, Work Longer.* Paris: Organisation for Economic Cooperation and Development.

Organisation for Economic Cooperation and Development. 2008. *Education at a Glance.* http:/www.oecd.org/edu/eag2007.

Poterba, James M. 1997. "Demographic Structure and the Political Economy of Public Education." *Journal of Policy Analysis and Management* 16(4): 48–66.

Poterba, James M. 1998. "Demographic Change, Intergenerational Linkages, and Public Education." *American Economic Review* 88(2): 315–20.

Robson, William. 2001. *Aging Populations and the Workforce: Challenges for Employers.* Winnipeg, Canada: British-North American Committee. http://www.cdhowe.org/pdf/BNAC_Aging_Populations.pdf.

Rosenbaum, James. 2001. *Beyond College for All: Career Paths for the Forgotten Half.* New York: Russell Sage Foundation.

Shoven, John, and Gopi Shah Godi. 2008. "Adjusting Government Policies for Age Inflation." Working Paper 14231. Cambridge, MA: National Bureau of Economic Research.

Song, Jae G. 2004. "Evaluating the Initial Impact of Eliminating the Retirement Earnings Test." *Social Security Bulletin.* 65(1): 1–15.

Strauss, Valerie. March 10, 2008. "Population Shift Sends Universities Scrambling." *Washington Post,* p. A01.

Toosi, Mira. 2006. "A New Look at Long-Term Labor Force Projections." *Monthly Labor Review* 129(11): 19–39.

Triest, Robert, Steven Sass, and Margarita Sapozhnikov. 2006. "Population Aging and the Structure of Wages." Boston: Center for

Retirement Research. http://escholarship.bc.edu/cgi/viewcontent. cgi?article=1114&context=retirement_papers.

U.S. Department of Education. 2006. *Digest of Education Statistics.* Washington, DC: National Center for Education Statistics. http://nces.ed.gov/Programs/digest.

U.S. Department of Education. 2007. *Digest of Education Statistics.* Washington, DC: National Center for Education Statistics. http://nces.ed.gov/Programs/digest.

Waldron, Hillary. 2007. "Trends in Mortality Differences and Life Expectancy for Male Social Security-Covered Workers by Socioeconomic Status." *Social Security Bulletin* 67(3): 1–28.

Wattenberg, Ben J. 2004. *Fewer: How the New Demography of Depopulation Will Shape Our Future.* Chicago: Ivan R. Dee.

Western Interstate Commission for Higher Education. 2008. *Knocking at the College Door.* Boulder, CO: WICHE.

World Bank. 2007. *World Development Indicators.* Washington, DC: World Bank.

Three

The Changing U.S. Family

No developments in the demography of developed countries are as challenging to explain and culturally controversial as the changes in the composition of families and households. Past patterns of near-universal marriage, of childbearing within marriage, of fertility above replacement levels, and of a low share of women in the labor market have given way to delays in marriage; declines in fertility; and high rates of divorce, nonmarital births, and female labor force participation. Some changes reinforce each other; delays in marriage, declining rates of marriage, and falling birth rates have encouraged more women to participate in the workforce.

This chapter begins by asking a number of questions about the changing dynamics of families, households, and living arrangements of children in the United States. How have family and household patterns changed over the last few decades? Are we witnessing a turn away from marriage or delays in marriage? Is cohabitation taking the place of marriage? What are the implications of changing marital status for the living arrangements and living standards of children? How different are U.S. trends from those in other developed countries?

The next section addresses the implications of changing families and households for people in their role as workers. How has the changing family affected the supply or workers, the stability of the workforce, and worker demand for job-related benefits? Given the linkages between social benefits and the organization of families, more workers are relying on public income support to supplement their wages. As a result, employers increasingly have to coordinate their actions with public agencies, such as child support collections and health insurance. In some cases, a wage increase will yield a smaller gain for workers because of associated reductions in public benefits.

The third section addresses how the family and household situations of children are exerting especially profound consequences for the nation's educational system. Schools are increasingly asked to reduce achievement gaps among students at the same time that parenthood patterns are increasingly unequal. The poverty associated with single-parenthood often directly influences schools through increased provision of free or reduced-price school lunch and breakfast programs. The indirect effects can be more serious, as children spend less time with parents and are more likely to experience household and geographic instability. In higher education, the diversity of economic challenges place added demands on public and private financial aid systems. On the other hand, reduced family size permits more parental investment per child and more space within households for children to do homework.

The evolution of families and households has already required responses by the nation's income support, job market, and educational systems. The concluding section looks ahead to see how the demographics of the family will continue to evolve and pose new challenges for workforce and educational policies.

DOCUMENTING AND INTERPRETING THE DEMOGRAPHICS OF FAMILIES AND HOUSEHOLDS

The definitions of "family" and "household" are not self-evident. The U.S. Census Bureau defines the family as consisting of two or more people sharing a home who are related by blood, marriage, or adoption. This definition excludes family members, even parents and children, who are living elsewhere. Also left out are cohabiting partners, unless they are the parent of a resident child. Households are made up of all persons sharing a residence, whether or not they are related. Although the family is always in a household and often the family and household is made up of the same persons, some households do not include families. Good examples are people living alone or with only unrelated persons. Finally, some people live in institutional settings like jails and are neither in Census families nor households.

Since 1960, the number of U.S. households more than doubled from about 53 to 116 million. At the same time, households have become increasingly diverse. In 1960, households with married couples made up nearly 74 percent of all households; by 2007, married couple households represented only half. Of the 63 million additional households, less than 20 million were married-couple households. Nonfamily households—which made up 15 percent of all households in 1960—accounted for nearly half of the increase in households. About 80 percent of the added nonfamily households were made up of one person. By 2003, men or women living alone accounted for over one in four households, up from 17 in 1970 (Fields 2004). A major component of this trend is the rising share of the elderly living alone (Kramarow 1995). With people living longer, more older people are forming separate households instead of living within the traditional family.[1] As the share of single-person households increased, the average size of households and families dropped 26 percent, from 3.33 persons in 1960 to 2.56 in 2007.

Families have become smaller as well, mainly because of the decline in the number of children. Since 1960, the average number of people per family fell by about 12 percent from 3.54 to 3.13 persons; on average, the number of children (individuals younger than 18 years old) was only 0.83 per family in 2007, down from 1.33 in 1960. Looking only at families with their own children, we see a similar decline over the same period from 2.33

to 1.81 children under 18 (U.S. Bureau of the Census 2008).[2] The decline in children under 18 was similar for both married couple and single-parent families with children.

CHANGES IN MARRIAGE, COHABITATION, AND THE LIVING ARRANGEMENTS OF CHILDREN

Shifts in social mores have been closely connected with changing patterns of marriage as well as childbearing. Over the first half of the 20th century, people were marrying at high rates and at younger ages; the median marriage age fell from about 26 to 23 for men and from 22 to 20 for women (Yaukey, Anderson, and Lundquist 2007). The picture changed dramatically after 1960. From 1960 to 2007, the median age at first marriage rose from 22.8 to 27.5 for men and from 20.3 to 25.6 for women (U.S. Bureau of the Census, Table MS-1, 2008). The striking delays in marriage affected whites as well as African-Americans. Between 1970 and 2000, the percent married at age 30 fell from 85 to 58 percent among white men and from 72 to 38 percent among African-American men.

The delays and declines in marriage have coincided with sharp increases in cohabitation. Between 1977 and 2006, the number of cohabiting couples heading their own households jumped fivefold, from under 1 million to over 5 million. When the Census counts all cohabiting couples, including those not heading a household, the figure reaches 6.5 million in 2007.[3] Using this figure, cohabiting couples make up about 10 percent of the couples living together as married or cohabiting and 8.7 percent of couples with children.

Cohabitation has become the norm for young people. Experiencing cohabitation prior to marriage rose from only 10 percent of those reaching age 20 in the 1950s to 65 percent of those reaching 20 in the mid-1980s to mid-1990s (Galston 2008). Although 89 percent of women and 83 percent of men are projected to marry at some point in their lives, these figures represent a significant decline from the early 1970s, when the proportions were about 96 percent.

Once married, people are less likely to stay married than in the past. Divorce and separation became increasingly acceptable and increasingly common. Of first marriages taking place in the 1955–1959 period, about 14 percent had become disrupted within 10 years. The proportion of disrupted marriages more than doubled to 31 percent by the early 1980s (Bramlett and Mosher 2002). At that peak divorce period, more than 40 percent of marriages ultimately were ending in divorce. Since then, divorce trends have largely stabilized at this high level.

As fewer people were getting married at each age group, married women were having fewer children. The fertility rate, the number of children born per 1,000 married women, declined from about 153 in 1960 to 88 by 2003 (National Center for Health Statistics 2003). At the same time, the tendency to delay or to avoid marriage combined with a rising fertility rate among unmarried women. For each 1,000 unmarried women, the number of births rose from 26.4 in 1970 to 43.7 in 2002.

One analysis finds that young people are delaying first marriages and instead increasingly cohabiting, partly because the availability of birth control pills led to a separation of sexual activity from marriage and a reduced tendency for "shotgun" marriages—as men feel less pressured to legitimize a birth by marrying a partner who they made pregnant (Akerlof, Yellen, and Katz 1996). The pill and legalized abortion have allowed women to have premarital sex with little risk of unwanted childbearing. Moreover, when women become pregnant, they are considered largely responsible for unprotected sex, lessening the social obligation on male partners to marry them. Reinforcing these trends, the rising number and prevalence of unmarried and teenage mothers has itself contributed to a decline in the social stigma once associated with out-of-wedlock childbearing.

The rising tendency of childbearing to take place outside marriage has become an important concern. In the first two-thirds of the 20th century, nonmarital births were quite uncommon. Although births to unwed parents rose slightly between 1920 and 1960, they reached only 5 percent of births by 1960 (Cutwright 1973). During these four decades, non-marital births did increase among nonwhites from about 12.5 to 21 percent (Cutwright 1973). In 1965, then Labor Department official (and later Senator) Daniel Patrick Moynihan expressed deep concern over the state of the black family in an official Labor Department report, citing this rise in unwed births, high rates of divorce, and high proportions of children growing up in mother-headed families (Moynihan 1967).

The concerns expressed by Moynihan over the changing structure of black families become far more widespread and vastly magnified over the next 40 years. For all Americans, rates of marriage declined, divorce rates increased, and the proportion of births to unwed parents multiplied. As Figure 3.1 shows, the share of births jumped from 5 percent in 1960 to over one-third by the early 1990s. In 2006, unwed births reached a new high at 38.5 percent of all births, or about seven times the 1960 rate

FIGURE 3.1
Unwed Births as a Share of All Births: 1950–2004

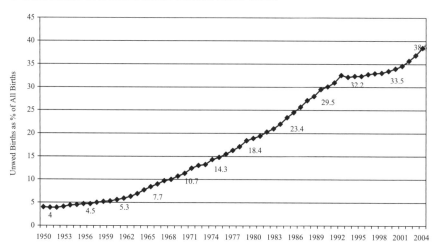

Source: Vital Statistics of the United States, Volume 1, Natality. Table 1-17; Martin et al. (2006), Table 18; Martin et al. (2007), Table 18; Hamilton et al. (2007), Table 7. National Center for Health Statistics. www.cdc.gov/nchs/births.htm

(Hamilton, Martin, and Ventura 2007). Of the 4.27 million children born in 2006, 1.64 million were born to unwed parents. The upward trend in nonmarital births has resulted from the decline in marriage, but also because of the increasing fertility rates among unmarried women of childbearing ages (Figure 3.2).

Some of these trends are benign and reflect the increasing equality of women. The increasing roles of women in higher education and the workforce and the sexual revolution have contributed to widespread changes in family and household patterns (Ellwood and Jencks 2004). Between 1960 and 2007, the labor force participation rate of adult women (ages 25–54) rose from 40 percent to over 75 percent. The share of adult women who graduated from college jumped from about 7 percent to 33 percent over the same period.[4] Moreover, women with a college degree are much more likely to work.

FIGURE 3.2
Rising Nonmarital Births and Birth Rates: 1980–2006

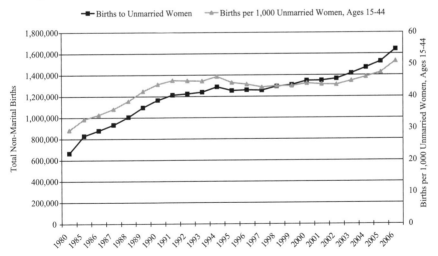

Source: *Vital Statistics of the United States,* Volume 1, Natality. Table 1-18; Martin, et al. (2006), Table 19; Martin et al. (2007); and Hamilton et al. (2007) page 1. National Center for Health Statistics. www.cdc.gov/nchs/births.htm

College-educated men and women still ultimately marry and delay childbearing until they do. Of all births to women with a BA or more, only about 7 percent were to unmarried couples.[5] Unfortunately, many of the family formation patterns raise serious concerns, especially for less-educated and low-income populations. Among less-educated women, childbearing is becoming increasingly separated from marriage. In 2005, over half of births to mothers with no more than a high school degree were outside marriage; in contrast, unwed births represented only about 8 percent of births to women with at least a college degree.[6] Divorce patterns vary sharply by education as well. More-educated women are becoming less likely to divorce, while among less-educated women, the divorce rates are high and increasing (Ellwood and Jencks 2004; Martin 2006; Raley and Bumpass 2003) Comparing marital dissolution rates within 10 years of marriage by year of first marriage (1975–1979 to 1990–1994), Martin (2006) found divorce increased from 38.3 to 46.3 percent among women with less than a high school degree but declined from 29.0 to 16.5 percent among women with a high school diploma.

Many other countries have also experienced high and rising rates of nonmarital childbearing. In 1960, nonmarital births were low in nearly all European countries; for example, the percentages of nonmarital births were 6 percent in France, 5 percent in the United Kingdom, 6 percent in Germany, and an average of about 8 percent in Scandinavian countries (Lerman and Ooms 1993). Today, in France and several Scandinavian countries, nonmarital births account for more than half of all births. These high rates arouse less concern than in the United States because they are generally associated with stable two-parent families in long-term cohabiting status. Despite rates of nonmarital childbearing of 40 to 50 percent, the proportion of children living with only one parent is 15 percent in France, 23 percent in Sweden, 21 percent in Norway, and 24 percent in the United Kingdom (Skinner, Bradshaw, and Davidson 2007).

In the United States, while many children born outside marriage begin with the involvement of both parents, the unwed parental relationships are often unstable. At the time of their child's birth, over 80 percent of unmarried men are either living with the child's mother (53 percent) or in a close romantic relationship with her (30 percent). But, by the time their children are 5 years old, less than 40 percent are closely linked with the child's mother, either as a spouse (16 percent), a cohabitant (18 percent), or in a close romantic relationship (5 percent) (Fragile Families Research Brief 2007). Of the mothers who were cohabiting with their child's father at the birth, only 34 percent were living with him 5 years later, and only 21 percent were steadily living together over the 5 year period (Carlson 2007). In contrast, over 80 percent of couples who were married when their child was born are stable and are living together through the child's first five years.

Children live in a variety of family and household contexts, as Figure 3.3 illustrates. As of 2002, about 60 percent of

FIGURE 3.3
Living Arrangements of All Children and Low-Income Children: 2002

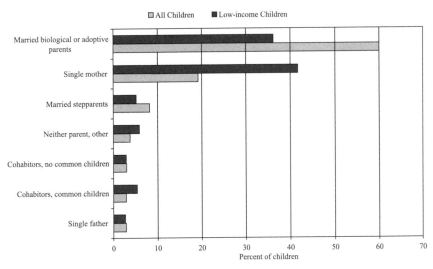

Source: Acs and Nelson (2003)

children under the age of 18 lived with married biological or adoptive parents; an additional 8 percent lived with a biological/adoptive parent and a married stepparent.[7] Only 3 percent lived with biological cohabiting parents, another 3 percent with single fathers, and another 4 percent with neither parent. Even among children under age 6, 25 percent were already living with only one or no biological parent. The proportions vary dramatically by race and income class. Among children living in the lowest income families (bottom 20 percent), only about 41 percent lived with both biological parents; the figure was even lower among black children (Lerman 2002a).

The marital and household status of single parents add further complexities that bear on the economic capacity of the family. Of single parents not cohabiting, one-third includes at least one other adult besides the parent. These arrangements potentially allow the parent to share responsibilities for home and work tasks. Another economically relevant issue is marital status. Compared to never-married mothers, single parents who were once married but are now divorced or separated are more likely to have built-up assets and more likely to obtain financial help through child support payments and voluntary support. Their children are more likely to have spent several years with and have a closer connection with the noncustodial parent. Unfortunately, children are increasingly likely to live with never-married single parents. Between 1968 and 2006, there was a 10-fold increase in the share of all children who were living with a never-married mother, from less than 1 percent in 1968 to over 10 percent in 2006. These children now make up more than 36 percent of children in single-parent households, up from 5 percent in 1968.

ECONOMIC AND SOCIAL IMPACTS ON FAMILIES AND CHILDREN

Shifts in marital patterns in the United States are helping to generate "Diverging Destinies" for children (McLanahan 2004), with children from married, two-parent families thriving and children from less-advantaged, single-parent families facing serious obstacles. McLanahan (2008) found that nonmarital childbearing reduces mobility and reproduces poverty from the parent to the child generation. The primary mechanisms for this pattern are what McLanahan calls *partnership instability* and *multi-partner fertility*. The mother's search for a long-term partner creates stress for mothers and children and leads to jealousy and mistrust by the other biological parent. Defined as men or women having children with different partners, multi-partner fertility causes fathers to spread their time and money across several children and can generate problems between past and current partners. With multi-partner fertility accompanying the unwed childbearing and with unwed parenthood rising much more among less-educated than among more-educated mothers, changing family patterns are apparently lowering economic mobility in the United States.

Even in the absence of intergenerational impacts, rising rates of nonmarital births and single parenthood have contributed significantly to the weak progress against poverty and to the rising rates of inequality among families with children. According to official poverty measures for 2007, nearly 37 percent of single-mother families were poor, compared with about 6.7 percent of married-couple families with children.[8] The gap is wider among black families. The poverty rate of black, single-mother families was 44 percent, a rate over five times the 8 percent rate experienced by black, married-couple families with children. The poverty differentials are nearly as high among Hispanic families, with poverty rates at 47 percent for single-mother families and 16 percent for two-parent families. Although Hispanic poverty rates were higher for each family type than the respective rates among black families, Hispanic families with children had somewhat lower overall rates than black families, because two-parent families are more common among Hispanics.

Differences in poverty rates persist with an income definition that incorporates taxes, tax credits, and many social benefits not included in the official poverty definition. Under this definition, only 3 percent of married couple families with children are counted as poor in 2007, compared to 22 percent of mother-headed families. As Figure 3.4 shows, family structure changes between 1974 and 2007 were associated with a rise in the official poverty rate of families with children. This rate rose from about 12 to 15 percent, but would have declined slightly had the rise in single-parent families not taken place. In some ways, the results in Figure 3.4 understate the full impact of family change because of the rising share of children living never-married parents, who are considerably more likely to fall below poverty than children with single parents who were once married.

A common objection to the idea that marriage enhances economic well-being is that the men whom current single mothers would marry are often poor themselves, and their marriage would leave the children in poverty in any case (Edin 2000; Ooms 2002). Lerman (1996) simulated what would happen to the current family income of single mothers if their tendency

FIGURE 3.4
Poverty Rates of Families: Actual and without Family Structure Change

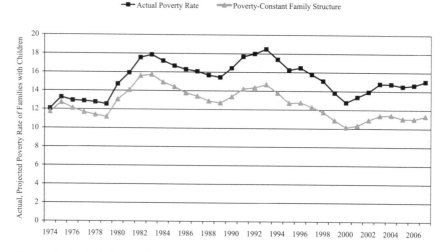

Source: Authors' tabulations based on U.S. Census Bureau official poverty rates by family structure. www.census.gov/hhes/poverty/histpov/histpovtb.html.

to marry in 1989 was the same as in 1971 and they married available men with similar levels of education, race-ethnic origin, and age. A recent study by Thomas and Sawhill (2002) replicated this approach for women in 1999. Although the couples in simulated marriages have incomes considerably below those in actual marriages, declines in poverty and inequality associated with marriage are substantial. Lerman found that child poverty rates would have fallen from 17.1 percent to less than 15 percent in 1989 and that the added marriages would have prevented half of the rise in family income inequality. Thomas and Sawhill project that the simulated marriages would have reduced the child poverty rate from about 17 to about 13 percent.

Another study of the economic impacts of marriage looked only at women with similar family backgrounds, all of whom had premarital first pregnancies leading to a birth (Lerman 2002b).[9] Of these mothers, those who married before the birth or in the year after this first birth subsequently had at least double the living standards of mothers who started out cohabiting or not living with the child's father. The improvements in living standards and reduced income volatility extended to black women and to women with the lowest academic test scores.

IMPLICATIONS FOR THE WORKFORCE

Major shifts in family formation and household arrangements have already interacted with the workforce and will continue to do so. Causation is often difficult to determine because changes in access to jobs can affect family patterns, just as family change influences labor force patterns and earnings. As women have increasingly gained access to jobs as physicians, lawyers, and high-level business positions, many have delayed marriage and childbearing. A weak job market for low-skill men may have reduced the likelihood that they marry the mother of their child. This section focuses on the trends in both family structure and workforce patterns, along with brief looks at the underlying causes, the role of public policy, and prospects for the future.

Women's increasing participation in the formal labor market is taking place alongside but only partly linked to the changing demographics of the family. Consider the rapid increases in labor force participation of 25- to 54-year-old women, a group that traditionally has focused on childrearing and other housework, relying on the earnings of a husband for the family's cash resources. Between 1960 and 2008, the labor force participation of women in this group jumped from 43 percent to 76 percent. Today, about three of four 25- to 54-year-old women are working; one in five working women are in part-time jobs. At the same time, men reduced their commitment to the labor force (from about a 97 to a 90 percent rate of participation), despite their traditional role as the main breadwinner of the family.

Demographic patterns are among the likely candidates contributing to the rising work levels of women. These include are delays in marriage, declines in the number of children, and increases in the share of mothers unable to rely on a husband or partner. Much of the increased labor force activity is among married women, especially married women with children. Only 17 percent married women participated in the workforce in 1948. By 1995, the labor force rate of married women had risen to 70 percent; since then, it has remained at that level or declined slightly. The decline in the number of children and other demographic factors apparently explain only about 20 percent of the added work activity of married women (Leibowitz and Klerman 1995). Instead, the key factors for married women are probably improved job opportunities, increased educational attainment, and changing social norms. Married women were responsive to wage increases in the 1980s, but less so in the 1990s (Blau and Kahn 2007). Moreover, higher wages for husbands did little to raise their work levels.

Figure 3.5 shows two groups of women sharply increasing their employment levels over the last 37 years.[10] First, we see

FIGURE 3.5
Women's Annual Weeks Worked: 1970 and 2007

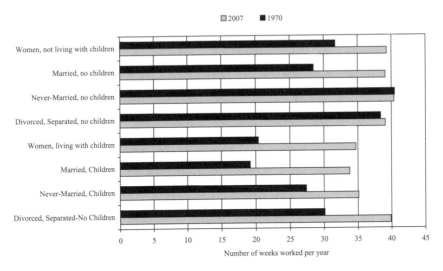

Source: Authors' tabulations of data from the 1971 and 2008 Current Population Surveys.

sharp increases in average weeks worked per year among married women with no children at home—an increase from 28.5 in 1970 to 39.1 in 2007 (those not working are included as zeros). These figures represent a jump from 54.7 to 75.1 percent in the share working in the typical week. Over the same period, unmarried women without children worked about the same amount in 1970. Second, all groups of women with children increased their time at work. The increase was higher among married mothers (a 14-week or 56 percent gain) than among unmarried mothers.

Until recently, public policies generally acted as disincentives to work because of the high rates at which benefits are reduced when earnings of recipients increase. Particularly troublesome was the fact that the high rates at which public benefits are phased out with income could result in marginal tax rates of 60 to 70 percent and beyond. Since the trend was away from marriage and toward single-parenthood, a big group of potential workers was negatively affected. In recent years, the public sector has restructured key benefits to lower the disincentive to work.

The change associated with the welfare reforms and improved work incentives spearheaded by large increases in the Earned Income Tax Credit (EITC) apparently generated some of the increased work effort among unmarried mothers, especially never-married mothers. Average weeks worked among never-married mothers had dropped between 1970 and 1985, but then jumped between 1985 and 2007. Between the early 1990s and early 2002, when states began implementing changes in the welfare system and the federal government began expanding the EITC, increasing numbers of unmarried mothers entered the workforce (Meyer and Rosenbaum 2001). Moreover, despite predictions that few jobs would be available to increased numbers of single mothers in the workforce (Edelman 1997), their unemployment rates fell and their real wages rose sharply over this period (Lerman 2001). The gains were especially notable for the least-educated single mothers.

Family structure changes alone would have increased women's work activity modestly. Along with the actual 1970–2007 changes in the share of women in various marital and parental groups, suppose that women did not change their work activity *within* marital and parental groups. These family structure changes, especially the reduction in the share of women with children, would themselves have led to a modest increase in employment but only by about 14 percent. The actual increase in the women's employment was about 43 percent.

Men's current and changing work activity also modestly depends on marital and parental status. Over the 1970–2007 period, the average amount worked by 25- to 54-year-old men declined slightly (see Figure 3.6). Although men who work most—married men living with children under 18—showed an increase in weeks worked over the period, this group declined sharply as a share of prime-age men (from 63.8 to 38.1 percent). Divorced and separated men with children worked more as well. But, these increases did not offset the shift among men away from resident fatherhood and the slight decline in work by men who did not live with children. Our calculations indicate

FIGURE 3.6
Men's Annual Weeks Worked: 1970 and 2007

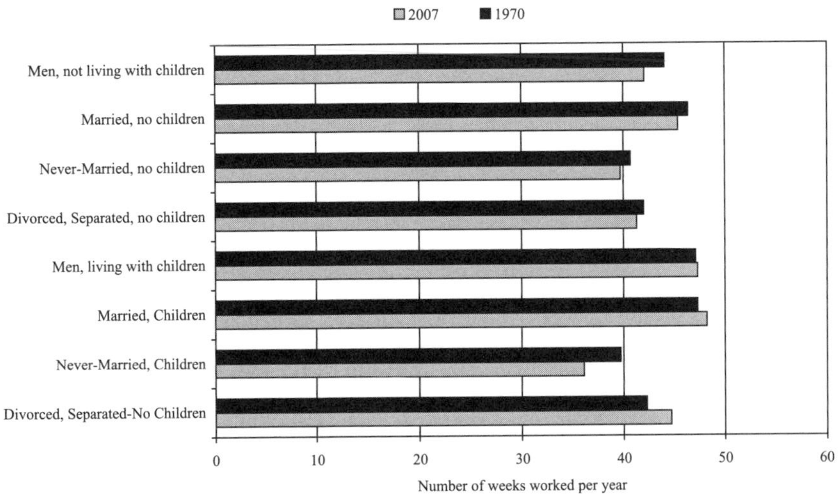

Source: Authors' tabulations of data from the 1971 and 2008 Current Population Surveys.

that, barring the family structure shift among men, men's weeks worked would not have declined.

For employers, changing demography and labor force participation patterns have strongly affected the make-up of their pool of prime-age workers in a given week. It is not simply a shift toward women in the workforce—women's share rose from 36 to 46 percent of all weeks worked over the 1970–2007 period. By far, the largest shift is that married men with children account for a sharply declining share of weeks worked, from 42 to 22 percent. Married men with or without children represented about 55 percent of all weeks worked in 1970, but only 34 percent in 2007. Counting married women along with men reveals the changing marital status of the workforce. In 1970, married women and men represented 81 percent of prime-age employment; by 2007, the proportion had fallen to 62 percent.

The increased entry of mothers in the job market—by married and unmarried mothers—has led to an increased demand for child care and a renewed emphasis on work–family issues. Between 1970 and 2007, the share of mothers working in a typical week increased from about 39 to 67 percent. Moreover, of mothers working in the labor market, the proportion with an average work week of 35 hours or more increased from 65 percent (in 1976) to 75 percent (in 2007). Thus, it is natural for child care concerns to increase. Yet, somewhat surprisingly, the typical prime-age worker was only a bit more likely to be a mother in 2007 than in 1970, a rise to 23 percent from 21 percent. One reason is fewer women are living with a child under 18—the percentage of 25- to 54-year-old women in this category declined from declined 68 to 53 percent.

The declining proportion of married men in the 25- to 54-year-old workforce is another notable pattern with implications for the labor market. Marriage raises the wage rates and hours worked of male workers, for reasons not entirely clear. The increases in work experience induced by marriage generate added human capital and thus a more productive labor force. In a recent article that takes account of the possibility that more productive people are more likely to marry, the marriage-induced gains in men's earnings are estimated at about 20 percent (Ahituv and Lerman 2007). These gains represent some improvement in the quality of hours worked (higher wages), as well as the number of hours worked. Reinforcing the main findings are results showing the negative impacts of divorce on wage rates and hours worked and the positive impacts of remarriage. Thus, for men, the shift away from stable marriage is exerting some influence on the labor market by lowering somewhat the labor supply, as well as the productivity of prime-age workers.

Another way in which demography can affect men's labor supply is through the payment of child support. Improvements in determining paternity of unwed fathers, obtaining support awards, and collecting payments have lessened the government burden of helping single parents but might reduce or stimulate work effort. For noncustodial parents who face high current or past obligations, about 25 to 50 percent of earned income is commonly withheld by employers. The result may be to decrease work effort, because of the fall in the worker's net wage after taxes and support payments (Holzer, Offner, and Sorensen 2005). The stimulus to work effort comes when non-custodial parents try to offset lost income to the child support system by working more. Employers have become increasingly part of the child support collection process, as all couples are required to withhold resources for the provision of child support.

IMPLICATIONS FOR EDUCATION

Trends in family structure have important implications for the nation's education systems, playing central roles education finance as well as student achievement and attainment.

The rise in single-parenthood and its associated lower income levels and higher poverty rates have contributed to an expansion of benefits under a variety of federal and state assistance programs for low-income students. Among the largest of these programs is the National School Lunch Program. It served 7.1 million children when it began in 1946, but today, more than 30.5 million students receive free- or reduced-price lunches at a cost of $8.7 billion per year. A related program, the School Breakfast Program, was added in 1969. Costing $2.1 billion per year, the program provides free- or reduced-price breakfasts to about 10 million students (U.S. Department of Agriculture 2008).

Education and day care programs designed to address the needs of working parents have also expanded along with women's increased labor force participation. Enrollment in pre-Kindergarten classes has increased dramatically. The percentage of 3- to 5-year-olds enrolled in such programs has increased from 27 percent in 1965 to more than 65 percent today, as shown in Figure 3.7. The most dramatic increase occurred between 1965 and 1975, as women—and particularly married women with children—entered the workforce in record numbers. Pre-K enrollment has grown steadily since, following the pattern of

FIGURE 3.7

Percent of 3-, 4-, and 5-Year-Old Children Enrolled in Preprimary Programs and Women's Labor Force Participation Rates: 1965–2010

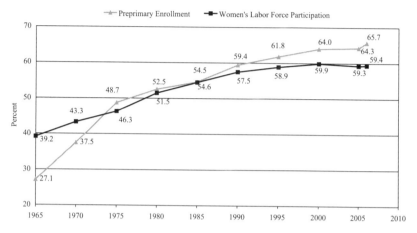

Source: U.S. Department of Education (2007) and U.S. Bureau of Labor Statistics, Table A-1 www.bls.gov/webapps/legacy/cpsatab1.htm.

increasing women's labor force participation. The slight surge in the late 1990s may reflect effects of the 1996 Welfare Reform as well as expansions in public preschool programs, such as Head Start. As of 2000, 62.8 percent of all women with children under age 6 worked outside of the home, and an even higher 65.3 percent of single mothers with young children were in the workforce (Blau and Currie 2004), making quality child care and preschool education a primary policy concern.

For school-age children, the growth in maternal employment has increased participation in after-school programs and extended day care programs. Traditional Kindergarten classes have expanded their hours—many moving from half- to full-day programs, in part to accommodate the schedules of working parents (DiMassa 2003). In later grades, afterschool enrichment programs have become essential elements of both public and private education: 28 percent of all families with children ages 5 to 14 consider "organized activities"—rather than parental, relative, or nonrelative care—as their primary child care arrangement outside of school.

The implications of these extensions of the school day are wide ranging. While these programs (especially public programs) reduce day care expenses and allow more time for work—and therefore earnings gains for working families—the programs do come at a cost to taxpayers and often require further expansion of related programs. In fact, the National School Lunch Program was recently extended to include support for snacks served to students in afterschool programs (U.S. Department of Agriculture 2008). Further, the impact of these programs on children's educational achievement and attainment is not yet clear.

Reviewing the evidence on afterschool programs, Kane (2004) finds no evidence of achievement gains for participating students in the year following participation, but he does find consistent evidence of enhanced student engagement in school and greater commitment to homework. Among Kane's most surprising findings, however, is that afterschool programs appear to increase parental involvement in school-related activities. Kane reports that parents were more likely to attend parent-teacher meetings, afterschool events, and open houses in all of the studies he reviewed—even those controlling for parental characteristics with random assignment.

In contrast to the somewhat mixed evidence on afterschool programs, nearly all studies of preschool and other early childhood education programs show unambiguously positive effects on academic achievement, educational attainment, and future earnings of students, particularly in the longer-term (for a review of this literature, see Blau and Currie 2004). These effects are evident even in large-scale public programs such as Head Start, a federally funded preschool program for low-income children (Blau and Currie 2004; Currie and Thomas 1995; Garces, Currie, and Thomas 2002; Ludwig and Phillips 2007). Undertaking a cost-benefit analysis of the program, Ludwig and Phillips (2007) find that Head Start yields long-term benefits in student achievement that more than offset the program's $9 billion of annual costs. Evidence on other early investments in human capital, especially intensive preschool programs, suggests that these programs generate much greater returns than educational investments later in the life course, both for the participants themselves and for society as a whole (Carneiro and Heckman 2003). These findings are helping to fuel the current movement for universal pre-Kindergarten.

Patterns of family formation and structure have clear implications for education policy and public finance—and these indirectly affect education and learning—as in the earlier examples. At a more micro level, however, a child's home environment exerts a direct influence on her academic achievement and attainment. Indeed, there is undoubtedly a strong correlation between family structure and academic performance (see for example, McLanahan and Sandefur 1994; Biblarz and Rafferty 1999; and Ginther and Pollack 2004), but results from causal studies of the impact of family structure on children's education are much less consistent (Ginther and Pollack 2004; Ermisch and Francesconi 2001; Gennetian 2005).

Among the most influential works, McLanahan and Sandefur (1994) find that children in single-parent families and those in blended stepfamilies have similar—and lower—educational attainment, compared with children living with both biological parents, although it is hard to determine causation. Children who grow up with both of their biological parents in the household are more likely to graduate from high school, more likely to attend college, and more likely to graduate from college. Other correlational studies reveal that children in living in single-parent and stepfamilies have lower grade point averages, poorer attendance records, and more problems with school authorities than students living in traditional nuclear families (Astone and McLanahan 1994; Thomson, Hanson, and McLanahan 1994). Using a slightly different classification, children experiencing a parental divorce score about a quarter of standard deviation lower on standardized tests than children living in traditional two-parent families (Amato 2001).

Much of this effect comes through differences in income and parental education levels between family types (Biblarz and

Rafferty 1999; Ginther and Pollack 2004). In fact, income may explain a full 50 percent of the achievement gap between single-parent and traditional nuclear families (Astone and McLanahan 1994). But it is not income alone that drives these differences. Parental involvement in children's education and residential mobility may also play important roles in driving the perceived differences in educational achievement and attainment (Astone and McLanahan 1994). Children raised by a single, working parent are likely to receive less help with homework, less supervision, and less interaction with parents than their peers in dual-parent households, although findings on the importance of parental involvement varies across studies (McLanahan and Sandefur 1994). Residential mobility may further exacerbate differences in achievement, particularly for children in blended families. Astone and McLanahan (1994) report that just 27 percent of children in nuclear families experienced at least one residential move between grades 5 and 10, compared to 53 percent of children in stepfamilies. Further, they find that residential mobility accounts for approximately 30 percent of the difference in high school dropout rates between these groups of students.

The nature of the event leading to the change in family structure may also help explain academic performance by family type. Interestingly, parental absence due to a death appears to have a much smaller impact on children's outcomes than divorce (Biblarz and Gottainer 2000; Corak 2001; and Lang and Zagorsky 2001), but the difference is not necessarily attributable to divorce per se. More likely, families that eventually divorce are likely to have other problems that contribute to poor student performance. As Cherlin (1999) and Cherlin, Chase-Landsdale, and McRae (1998) point out, students who perform poorly in school after a divorce typically performed poorly before the divorce as well, suggesting that any number of other factors relating to the home environment, such as parental stress or discord, may have a greater effect on educational outcomes than single-parenthood itself. Studies that control for these and other potentially confounding factors find much smaller and often insignificant differences in educational outcomes by family structure (Ginther and Pollack 2004; Biblarz and Rafferty 2001; Gennetian 2005), suggesting that family structure may not exert an independent causal effect on education achievement. Nonetheless, to the extent that family structure is correlated with a host of other characteristics associated with lower academic performance and attainment, an understanding of the changing nature of the U.S. family can help educators and policymakers address the challenges faced by a new generation children.

While many of the changes in family structure described earlier are likely to have negative implications for students, parents, and schools, other recent trends will have positive effects on the U.S. education system. Declining fertility will reduce elementary and secondary enrollments, perhaps relieving pressures on school district budgets. Yet, it is unlikely that this effect will be strong enough to outweigh increases due to natural population growth and immigration. A more noticeable effect of declining fertility, however, may be improved educational attainment and achievement. With fewer children per household, parents can allocate more resources to each child.

Famously, work by Becker (1960) and by Becker and Lewis (1973) posit that there exists a tradeoff between the quantity and "quality" of children. Becker and Lewis contend that parents, facing limited budgets, time, and other resources, must spread these resources across their children. Having fewer children, then, implies that each child receives a larger share of those resources and a greater level of investment overall. This theory has particularly important implications for parental investments in education, or human capital. Considering only financial investments in human capital, parents with fewer children can spend more money per child, perhaps sending children to private schools, hiring special tutors, or undertaking other enrichment activities that they would not have undertaken if the same money was spread among more children. A parent's time may be even more valuable than money. With fewer children, parents can spend relatively more time helping with homework, talking to teachers, or otherwise getting involved in their child's education.

Empirical work generally supports the quantity-quality trade-off hypothesis. Hanushek (1992) finds that academic achievement growth—or the gain from year to year for an individual student—falls with increased family size, at least among the low-income black families that he studies. Extrapolating to the U.S. population more generally, Hanushek calculates that the shift to smaller family sizes between 1965 and 1985 may have increased performance on standardized tests by as much as 1.5 to 1.9 percent.

Compared to its impact on elementary and secondary education, the impact of changing family structure on postsecondary education is less obvious, but potentially important nonetheless. The lower educational attainment of children raised in single-parent and blended families may mean a decline in postsecondary enrollment, but this decline is likely to be more than made up for by the many other factors that drive college-going. For example, an economic slowdown may mean increased postsecondary enrollment as workers seek retraining. Added to this, the rising college wage premium and a slight increase in the traditional college-age population suggests continued enrollment increases, as described in the previous chapter.

Where the impacts of family structure may be most evident in postsecondary education is in their impact on financial aid programs. Many need-based aid programs, such as the federal Pell Grant program, calculate an "Expected Family Contribution (EFC)," or the amount that a student and her family should be able to contribute to her college education. This EFC is then compared to the cost of attendance to determine whether a student is eligible for a grant and its size. For dependent students, parental tax returns are used to calculate EFC. To the extent that children in single-parent families have lower income than others, the result could be a potentially large impact on financial aid. The effect on the Pell Grant program may be particularly strong since grant funding is guaranteed for students meeting the criteria (based on EFC and COA) set by the legislation.

As in the case of elementary and secondary education, however, declining fertility may have the opposite effect on financial aid programs. Following Becker's quantity-quality tradeoff, parents with fewer children should have more to spend on college education for each. In fact, most need-based aid programs, including the Pell Grant, take into account family size and the college attendance of siblings in determining the EFC: with fewer children per family, eligibility for Pell Grants may decline.

Perhaps most relevant to higher education and training is the rise in women's labor force participation and delayed childbearing. Together, as Figure 3.8 documents, these trends have fueled a boom in women's enrollment in postsecondary education and training programs, as well as rising degree completion.

FIGURE 3.8
Women's Enrollment as a Share of All Enrollment in Degree-Granting Institutions: 1945–2005

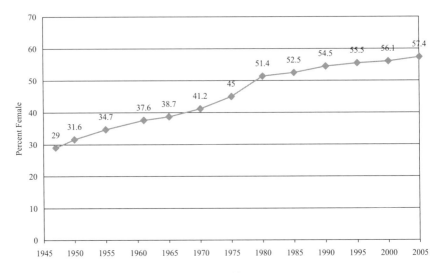

Source: U.S. Deparment of Education (2007), Table 179.

In 1947, women comprised just 29 percent of enrollment in degree-granting institutions. Today, women have become the majority, at 57 percent (U.S. Department of Education 2007) Degree attainment has similarly increased: rather than dropping out after obtaining the so-called "Mrs. degree" as in earlier decades, women make up a majority of degrees conferred among associate's, bachelor's, and master's degrees. As Figure 3.9 shows, gender differences in degree attainment are likely to increase further, with women receiving the majority of degrees at all levels of postsecondary education by 2016–2017.

Despite these gains, women still trail men in educational attainment along several dimensions. According to the 2000 Census, just 22.8 percent of all women age 25 and over have at least a bachelor's degree, compared to 26.1 percent of men. Similarly, women trail in advanced degrees—only 7.8 percent of women hold a master's, professional, or doctoral degree versus 10 percent of men (U.S. Bureau of the Census 2002, Table 2). Gender gaps in math and science advanced degrees are

FIGURE 3.9
Percentage of Degrees Conferred to Women: 1969–70, 1999–00, and 2016–17

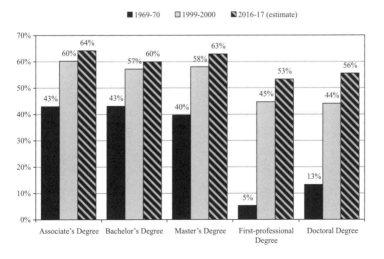

Source: U.S. Department of Education (2007), Table 258.

particularly large. Women receive less than 30 percent of all mathematics doctoral degrees and 43 percent of science doctoral degrees, contributing to the continued underrepresentation of women in medicine and academia (see Figure 3.10). On the other hand, women make up the vast majority of science-based associate's degrees, reflecting women's overrepresentation in lower-skilled fields, such as medical assistance.

What accounts for these differences? The answer is complex, but issues of family and household responsibility likely play a central role. Despite increasing gender equity, women today continue to take on a larger share of child care and housework than their husbands and partners—particularly among married couples (e.g., Hersch and Stratton 1997; Achen and Stafford 2005; Davis, Greenstein, and Marks 2007). The struggle to balance work and family continues with this generation, and the growing importance of a college education presents further challenges in achieving that balance. Access to affordable, high-quality child care, reasonable leave policies, and flexible scheduling are not only important in supporting women in the workplace, but such policies can and should be considered in the context of higher education as well. Two-year colleges have

FIGURE 3.10
Percentage of Math and Science Degrees Conferred to Women: 2006

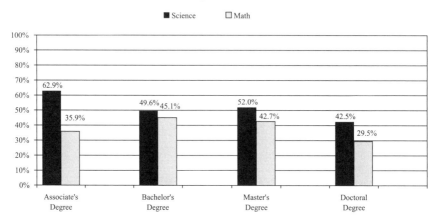

Source: Authors' tabulations of data from U.S.Department of Education (2007).

already made strides in this area, but four-year, masters', professional, and doctoral programs could push further in their support of working parents of both sexes.

CONCLUSIONS

The past several decades have witnessed dramatic changes in the structure of American families. With rising divorce rates, single-parenthood, and cohabitation outside of marriage, families today are more fractured and more dynamic than ever before. Collectively, we will experience a much wider variety of family and household living arrangements over our lifetimes than any generation in history, as stepfamilies, half-siblings, second marriages, and many other nonnuclear family structures become more common. Declining fertility rates, delayed childbearing, and increased women's labor force participation are trends that serve to both reinforce and offset the effects of other changes in family structure. Together, patterns of family formation will present both challenges and opportunities for our workforce and education system. What is clear in both areas is that employers, teachers and administrators, and policymakers must consider the needs of a growing number of working parents in the years to come.

NOTES

1. Tabulations by authors from Bureau of the Census, Households and Families Data, Tables HH-1 and FM-1. See http://www.census.gov/population/www/socdemo/hh-fam.html.

2. These figures come from Tables HH-4 and Tables FM-3. See http://www.census.gov/population/www/socdemo/hh-fam.html.

3. These figures come from Table UC-1, accessed through the U.S. Census Bureau Web site at http://www.census.gov/population/socdemo/hh-fam/uc1.xls.

4. These figures come from Table A-1, accessed through the U.S. Census Bureau Web site at http://www.census.gov/population/www/socdemo/educ-attn.html.

5. Authors' tabulations from the National Vital Statistics System, National Center for Health Statistics, Centers for Disease Control and Prevention, http://209.217.72.34/VitalStats/ReportFolders/report Folders.aspx.

6. These results come from unpublished tables available through the National Vital Statistics System, National Center for Health Statistics, http://209.217.72.34/VitalStats/TableViewer/tableView.aspx.

7. These figures draw on data from the National Survey of America's Families, a nationally representative survey that offers more detailed family and household information than data reported by the U.S. Census Bureau. See http://www.urban.org/center/anf/2002methodology.cfm for a discussion of the methodology used in this survey.

8. The data for this paragraph comes from Tables POV04 at the U.S. Census Bureau Web site; see http://pubdb3.census.gov/macro/032008/pov/new04_100.htm.

9. For a review of the economic benefits of marriage, see Waite and Gallagher (2000).

10. All data in the next several paragraphs come from tabulations by the authors from the 1971, 1977, 1985, and 2008 Current Population Surveys.

REFERENCES

Achen, Alexandra C., and Frank P. Stafford. 2005. "Data Quality of Housework Hours in the PSID: Who Really Does the Dishes?" Panel Study of Income Dynamics Technical Working Paper No. 05-04.

Acs, Gregory, and Sandi Nelson. 2003. "Changes in Family Structure and Child Well-Being: Evidence from the 2002 National Survey of America's Households." Washington, DC: Urban Institute.

Ahituv, Avner, and Robert Lerman. 2007. "How Do Marital Status, Wage Rates, and Work Effort Interact?" *Demography* 44(3): 623–47.

Akerlof, George, Jane Yellen, and Lawrence Katz. 1996. "An Analysis of Out-of-Wedlock Childbearing in the United States." *Quarterly Journal of Economics* 111(2): 277–317.

Amato, Paul R. 2001. "Children of Divorce in the 1990s: An Update of the Amato and Keith (1991) Meta-Analysis." *Journal of Family Psychology* 15(3): 355–70.

Astone, Nan Marie, and Sara S. McLanahan. 1994. "Family Structure, Residential Mobility, and School Dropout: A Research Note." *Demography* 31(4): 575–84.

Becker, Gary S. 1960. "An Economic Analysis of Fertility." In *Demographic and Economic Change in Developed Countries.* Universities—National Bureau Conference Series, No. 11. Princeton, NJ: Princeton University Press (for NBER).

Becker, Gary S., and H. Gregg Lewis. 1973. "On the Interaction Between Quantity and Quality of Children." *Journal of Political Economy* 81(2): S279–S288.

Biblarz, T. J., and A. E. Rafferty. 1999. "Family Structure, Educational Attainment, and Socioeconomic Success: Rethinking the 'Pathology of Matriarchy.'" *American Journal of Sociology* 105: 321–65.

Biblarz, T. J., and G. Gottainer. 2000. "Family Structure and Children's Success: A Comparison of Widowed and Divorced Single-Mother Families." *Journal of Marriage and Family* 62: 533–48.

Blau, David, and Janet Currie. 2004. "Preschool, Day Care, and After-School Care: Who's Minding the Kids?" NBER Working Paper No. 10670. Cambridge, MA: National Bureau of Economic Research.

Blau, Francie, and Lawrence Kahn. 2007. "Changes in the Labor Supply Behavior of Married Women, 1980–2000." *Journal of Labor Economics* 25(3): 393–438.

Bramlett, M. D., and W. D. Mosher. 2002. "Cohabitation, Marriage, and Remarriage in the United States." National Center for Health Statistics. *Vital Health Statistics* 23(22).

Carlson, Marcia. 2007. "Trajectories of Couple Relationship Quality after Childbirth: Does Marriage Matter?" Center for Research on Child Wellbeing Working Paper No. 2007-11-FF. Princeton, NJ: Fragile Families and Child Well-Being Study.

Carneiro, P., and J. J. Heckman. 2003. "Human Capital Policy." In *Inequality in America: What Role for Human Capital Policies?*, ed. J. J. Heckman and A.B. Krueger. Cambridge, MA: MIT Press.

Cherlin, Andrew J. 1999. "Going to Extremes: Family Structure, Children's Well-Being, and Social Science." *Demography* 36: 421–28.

Cherlin, Andrew J., P. L. Chase-Landsdale, and C. McRae. 1998. "Effects of Parental Divorce on Mental Health Throughout the Life Course." *American Sociological Review* 63: 239–49.

Corak, M. 2001. "Death and Divorce: The Long-Term Consequences of Parental Loss on Adolescents." *Journal of Labor Economics* 19: 682–715.

Currie, Janet, and Duncan Thomas. 1995. "Does Head Start Make a Difference?" *American Economic Review* 85(3): 341–64.

Cutwright, Phillip. 1973. "Illegitimacy and Income Supplements." In *The Family, Poverty, and Welfare Programs: Factors Influencing Family Instability.* Paper No. 12 (Part 1). Studies in Public Welfare. Joint Economic Committee. Washington, DC: U.S. Government Printing Office.

Davis, Shannon N., Theodore N. Greenstein, and Jennifer Gerteisen Marks. 2007. "Effects of Union Type on Division of Household Labor: Do Cohabiting Men Really Perform More Housework?" *Journal of Family Issues* 28(9): 1246–72.

DiMassa, Cara Mia. December 29, 2003. "Parents, Schools Are Learning to Like Full-Day Kindergarten." *Los Angeles Times*, A-1.

Edelman, Peter. 1997. "The Worst Thing Bill Clinton Has Done." *Atlantic Monthly* 279(3): 43–58.

Edin, Kathryn. 2000. "Few Good Men: Why Poor Mothers Don't Marry or Remarry." *American Prospect* 11(4): 26–31.

Ellwood, David T., and Christopher Jencks. 2004. "The Uneven Spread of Single-Parent Families: What Do We Know? Where Do We Look for Answers?" In *Social Inequality*, ed. Kathryn M. Neckerman. New York: Russell Sage Foundation, 3–77.

Ermisch, Z., and M. Francesconi. 2001. "Family Structure and Children's Achievements." *Journal of Population Economics* 14: 249–70.

Fields, Jason. 2004. "America's Families and Living Arrangements. 2003." In *Current Population Reports*. Washington, DC: U.S. Census Bureau, 20-553.

Fragile Families Research Brief. 2007. "Parents' Relationship Status Five Years after a Non-Marital Birth." Princeton, NJ: Princeton University, Center for Research on Child Wellbeing.

Galston, William. 2008. *The Changing Twenties.* Washington, DC: National Campaign to Prevent Teen and Unplanned Pregnancy.

Garces, Eliana, Janet Currie, and Duncan Thomas. 2002. "The Longer-Term Effects of Head Start" *American Economic Review* 92(4): 999–1012.

Gennetian, Lisa A. 2005. "One or Two Parents? Step or Half Siblings? The Effect of Family Structure on Young Children's Achievement." *Journal of Population Economics* 18: 415–36.

Ginther, Donna, and Robert A. Pollack. 2004. "Family Structure and Children's Educational Outcomes: Blended Families, Stylized Facts, and Descriptive Regressions." *Demography* 41(4): 671–96.

Hamilton, Brady, Joyce Martin, and Stephanie Ventura. 2007. "Births: Preliminary Data for 2006." *National Vital Statistics Reports* 56(7). www.cdc.gov/nhcs.

Hanushek, Eric A. 1992. "The Trade-off Between Child Quantity and Quality." *Journal of Political Economy* 100(11): 84–117.

Hersch, Joni, and Stratton, Leslie S. 1997. "Housework, Fixed Effects, and Wages of Married Workers." *Journal of Human Resources* 32(2): 285–307.

Holzer, Harry J., Paul Offner, and Elaine Sorensen. 2005. "Declining Employment among Young Black Less-Educated Men: The Role of Incarceration and Child Support." *Journal of Policy Analysis and Management* 24(2): 329–50.

Kane, Thomas J. 2004." The Impact of After-School Programs: Interpreting the Results of Four Recent Evaluations." New York: William T. Grant Foundation.

Kramarow, Elaine. 1995. "The Elderly Who Live Alone in the United States: Historical Perspectives on Household Change." *Demography* 32(3): 335–52.

Lang, K., and J. L. Zagorsky. 2001. "Does Growing Up with a Parent Absent Really Hurt?" *Journal of Human Resources* 36: 253–73.

Leibowitz, Arleen, and Jacob Klerman. 1995. "Explaining Changes in Married Mothers' Employment over Time." *Demography* 32(3): 365–78.

Lerman, Robert I. 1996. "The Impact of Changing U.S. Family Structure on Child Poverty and Income Inequality." *Economica* 63(250S): S119–S139.

———. 2001. "Less Educated Single Mothers Achieved High Wage and Employment Gains in the Mid 1990s." Washington, DC: Urban Institute Press.

———. 2002a. "How Do Marriage, Cohabitation, and Single Parenthood Affect the Material Hardships of Families with Children?" Washington, DC: Urban Institute Press.

————. 2002b. "Married and Unmarried Parenthood and the Economic Well-being of Families: A Dynamic Analysis of a Recent Cohort." Washington, DC: Urban Institute Press.

Lerman, Robert, and Theodora Ooms. 1993. "Introduction: Evolution of Unwed Fatherhood as a Policy Issue." In *Young Unwed Fathers: Changing Roles and Emerging Policies,* ed. Robert I. Lerman and Theodora Ooms. Philadelphia: Temple University Press.

Ludwig, Jens, and Deborah Phillips. 2007. "The Benefits and Costs of Head Start." NBER Working Paper No. W12973. Cambridge, MA: National Bureau of Economic Research.

Martin, Joyce A., Brady E. Hamilton, Paul D. Sutton, Stephanie J. Ventura, Fay Menacker, Sharon Kirmeyer, and Marth Munson. 2007. "Births: Final Data for 2005." *National Vital Statistics Reports* 5(6). www.cdc.gov/nhcs.

Martin, Joyce A., Brady E. Hamilton, Paul D. Sutton, Stephanie J. Ventura, Fay Menacker, and Sharon Kirmeyer. 2006. "Births: Final Data for 2004." *National Vital Statistics Reports* 55(1). www.cdc.gov/nhcs.

Martin, Steven. 2006. "Trends in Marital Dissolution by Women's Education in the United States." *Demographic Research* 15: 537–60.

McLanahan, Sara. 2004. "Diverging Destinies: How Children Are Faring under the Second Demographic Transition." *Demography* 41(4): 607–27.

————. 2008. "Fragile Families and the Reproduction of Poverty." Working Paper 2008-04-FF. Princeton, NJ: Fragile Families Research Project.

McLanahan, Sara, and Gary Sandefur. 1994. *Growing Up with a Single Parent: What Hurts, What Helps.* Cambridge, MA: Harvard University Press.

Meyer, Bruce, and Dan Rosenbaum. 2001. "Welfare, the Earned Income Tax Credit, and the Labor Supply of Single Mothers." *Quarterly Journal of Economics* 116(3): 1063–1114.

Moynihan, Daniel P. 1967. "The Negro Family: The Case for National Action." Reprinted in *The Moynihan Report and the Politics of Controversy,* ed. Lee Rainwater and William Yancey. Cambridge, MA: MIT Press.

National Center for Health Statistics. 2003. *Vital Statistics of the United States, 2003, Volume I, Natality*. Table 1-19. http://www.cdc.gov/nchs/data/statab/natfinal2003.annvol1_19.pdf.

Ooms, Theodora. 2002. "Marriage Plus." *American Prospect*, Spring, 4–9.

Raley, K., and L. Bumpass. 2003. "The Topography of the Divorce Plateau: Levels and Trends in Union Stability in the United States after 1980." *Demographic Research* 8: 245–59.

Skinner, C., J. Bradshaw, and J. Davidson. 2007. "Child Support Policy: An International Perspective." Department for Work and Pensions Research Report 405, Leeds: Corporate Document Services. http://www.dwp.gov.uk/asd/asd5/rports2007-2008/rrep405.pdf.

Thomas, Adam, and Isabel Sawhill. 2002. "For Richer or Poorer: Marriage as an Antipoverty Strategy." *Journal of Policy Analysis and Management* 21(4): 587–600.

Thomson, E., T. L. Hanson, and S. S. McLanahan. 1994. "Family Structure and Child Well-Being: Economic Resources vs. Parental Behaviors." *Social Forces* 73: 221–42.

U.S. Bureau of the Census. 2003. *Educational Attainment: Census 2000*. Census 2000 Brief. http://www.census.gov/prod/2003pubs/c2kbr-24.pdf.

U.S. Bureau of the Census. 2008. Table MS-1: Marital Status of the Population 15 Years Old and Over, by Sex and Race, 1950 to Present. http://www.census.gov/population/socdemo/hh-fam/ms1.xls.

U.S. Department of Agriculture. 2008. "National School Lunch Program Fact Sheet." Food and Nutrition Service. http://www.fns.usda.gov/cnd/Lunch/NSLPFactSheet.pdf.

U.S. Department of Education. 2007. *Digest of Education Statistics*. National Center for Education Statistics, http://nces.ed.gov/Programs/digest.

Waite, Linda J., and Maggie Gallagher. 2000. *The Case for Marriage*. New York: Doubleday.

Yaukey, David, Douglas Anderson, and Jennifer Hickes Lundquist. 2007. *Demography: The Study of Human Populations*. Long Grove, IL: Waveland Press.

Four

Rising Immigration

As John F. Kennedy famously pointed out, we are a nation of immigrants (Kennedy 1964). The vast majority of U.S. residents today can trace their roots back to another country of origin. Immigrants from every corner of the world—and their descendents—contribute to an ever more diverse melting pot that is the population of the United States. While the faces and languages of U.S. immigrants have changed over time, their reasons for immigrating remain largely the same: simply put, they come in search of a better life.

Today, debates over immigration policy have taken center stage in American politics, in the media, and around dinner tables across the country. The primary concern is an increasing number of immigrants entering or remaining in the country illegally. These undocumented or illegal immigrants (we use the terms interchangeably) are raising concerns over their possible impacts on the jobs and wages of native-born and legal immigrants, as well as their use of public resources and government assistance programs.

While today's immigration policy debates appear to some to be particularly heated, it is important to recognize that these debates are by no means new in American history. Racism and anxiety over the threat of cheap labor fueled the first anti-immigrant legislation in the late 19th century, leading to the Chinese Exclusion Act of 1882, which essentially prohibited immigration from China for a number of years. Policy debates continued into the 1920s with, among other changes, the introduction of a national-origin quota system in the Immigration Act of 1924. Interestingly, an unintended consequence of this system was the rise of illegal immigration—by Europeans. A report by the National Research Council points out that many Europeans who could not get into the United States through the quota system were able to enter the country illegally through Canada and Mexico in the 1920s and 1930s due to their lack of quotas (National Research Council 1997).

While immigration slowed during the Great Depression and World War II, one interesting policy stands out in this period. In a striking connection to policy options debated today, a temporary worker program was put in place in 1943 to allow agricultural workers from Mexico and other Latin American countries to obtain seasonal employment on U.S. farms. Later known as the Bracero Program, it remained in place until 1964. Perhaps even more heated than debates today, critics argued that the Bracero Program affected working conditions, job opportunities, and the wages of resident farmworkers (National Research Council 1997).

In 1965, the Immigration and Nationality Act Amendments abolished national-origin quotas, replacing them with quotas based on Western and Eastern hemisphere countries. More important, however, was a new preference for family unification and preferences for certain skills. The legislation was of extraordinary importance in shaping the subsequent scale and composition of immigration. The number of immigrants from developing countries increased rapidly, and the composition of immigrants changed substantially. Since the 1980s, most legislation has focused on the problem of illegal immigration, adding employer sanctions in 1986 and restricting access to public assistance benefits in 1996.

Since 1996, no comprehensive immigration legislation has passed, despite several major Congressional and Presidential initiatives. In 2005, a bipartisan bill sponsored by Ted Kennedy (D-MA) and John McCain (R-AZ), and supported by President Bush, failed to gain the support of the Republican Congress. A 2007 version of the bill did not pass in the Democratic Congress. Many argued that its provisions—including a guest worker program and a pathway to citizenship—did not do enough to enforce the borders. In the coming years, we can expect further changes in immigration policy, but whether these will come in the form of additional employer verification systems, guest worker programs, pathways to citizenship, or stronger border security is not clear.

These policy changes have played a critical role in shaping the size and mix of immigration to the United States. As in the past, today's immigrants have made their mark on social and cultural life and added to the diversity of America. Immigrants have become leading entrepreneurs, artists, physicians, scientists, and musicians. Refugees seeking political asylum have built new lives. Some groups of immigrants have helped revitalize sections of major cities (Bernstein 2007; Borges-Mendez, Gaston, Liu, and Watanabe 2005). Others have flooded the low-skill job market and provided labor for an underground economy (Borjas 2007). Although individual stories of struggle and of triumph or tragedy can be compelling, our focus is on three broad questions. First, how does immigration fit into the demographic picture of the United States? Second, what are the implications for the labor market and the educational system? Third, how have policymakers attempted to respond to these impacts? We begin with a review of the trends in immigration in their historic context.

THE UPS AND DOWNS OF IMMIGRATION

In 1850, the U.S. Census began collecting data on nativity— or country of birth (Gibson and Jung 2006). Since then, we have been able to track the changing number and proportion of U.S. residents that are "foreign-born." Although the number is about the best measure we have to judge the number of immigrants in the United States, the foreign-born classification does not distinguish between permanent versus temporary residents, citizens versus noncitizens, documented versus undocumented, nor refugees versus immigrants coming for economic and family reasons. In fact, the classification includes a small number of residents born overseas to American parents. Still, unless noted otherwise, we use the terms foreign-born and immigrant interchangeably in the remainder of the chapter.

What is most striking in looking at the U.S. Census Bureau's numbers is the sheer number of foreign-born residents in the United States. In 2000, the number of foreign-born residents stood at 31.3 million, the highest in our history. This number represents a threefold increase over the number of foreign-born individuals living here in 1900, at just 10.3 million (Gibson and Jung 2006).

Still, despite the large number of immigrants, the percentage of foreign-born residents today remains moderate by historical standards. Today, 11.1 percent of U.S. residents are immigrants, compared to 11.6 percent in 1930 and a high of almost 15 percent at the turn of the 20th century (Gibson and Jung 2006). The two lines in Figure 4.1 illustrate the differences between the trends in the number of immigrants and the proportion of immigrants in the population. While both statistics are informative, proportional measures probably do better in reflecting the importance and impact of immigrants in society. Both measures reveal a steep increase in the foreign-born population since 1970. After a record low proportion of immigrants in 1970 (4.7 percent), immigration increased rapidly in the decades since, in part due to the growth of undocumented immigrants. Between 1990 and 2000, the percentage of foreign-born residents jumped from 7.9 percent to 11.1 percent.

Focusing on the number of immigrants in the United States at a point in time masks substantial changes in the flows of immigration—a consideration that is particularly important for policy. In these terms, the peak year of legal immigration flow into the United States was 1907 when almost 1.3 million

FIGURE 4.1
U.S. Foreign-Born Population: 1850–2000

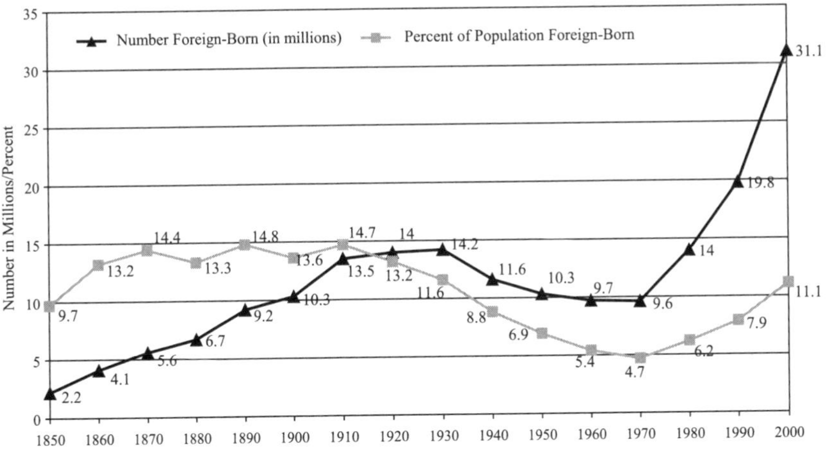

Source: Author's tabulations of data from Gibson & Jung (2007), Table 1.

foreign-born residents entered the country (National Research Council 1997). Again, however, a more telling figure would be a proportional measure of immigrant flow. Annual immigrants inflows per 1,000 residents today are just half of what they were in the early twentieth century—around 5 per 1,000 residents compared to 11 per 1,000 residents between 1900 and 1910 (National Research Council 1997).

The number of immigrants becoming permanent residents has increased rapidly in recent years. In 2006–2007, an average of 1.16 million foreign nationals became lawful permanent residents (obtained a "green card"), about a 50 percent increase over the 1998–2000 average of 713,000 (U.S. Department of Homeland Security 2007). About 60 percent of these individuals did not enter the United States in 2006–2007 but had their status converted to legal permanent resident in those years. In fact, the number of new permanent immigrants in a given year depends on the rate applications are processed, as well as the numbers of applicants. Of all new legal permanent residents, over 60 percent obtained their green cards as a result of being a family member of a citizen. About 14 percent became legal residents as a result of an employment-based preference. In 2007, nearly 130,000 of these immigrants entered the United States under a temporary employment visa and converted to permanent status. Green cards issued to refugees and those seeking asylum have more than doubled since the late 1990s. The annual number of refugees and asylees who became lawful permanent residents reached over 140,000 in 2006 and 2007, almost triple the average yearly level in 1998–2000.

So far, our numbers have ignored changes in the legal status of immigration. Although it is challenging for researchers to identify undocumented immigrants, there is no doubt that illegal immigration has increased in recent years. The most reliable and unbiased estimates of illegal immigration come from Jeffrey Passel and researchers at the Urban Institute and Pew Hispanic Center. They subtract the number of legal immigrants documented by the Department of Homeland Security from the number of noncitizens reported by the U.S. Census, Current Population Survey, and other official sources (Capps et al. 2005; Passel and Clark 1998; Passel 2006). Defining illegal immigration as illegal entry into the country (such as border crossings), overstaying visas (such as tourist or student visas), and other violations of the terms of their immigration status, Passel (2006) estimates that there are 11.5 to 12 million undocumented immigrants in the United States, with roughly 500,000 new undocumented immigrants entering or overstaying visas each year. Capps et al. (2005) report that undocumented immigrants now make up more than one in four immigrants; the figure was 28 percent of all immigrants in 2003. At 28 percent, the number of illegal immigrants is almost equal to the number immigrants who are naturalized citizens at 31 percent of the total (Capps et al. 2005, as shown in Figure 4.2).

A third group of immigrants come on temporary, employment-related visas. The largest group in this category are workers covered under the H-1B program, a visa program aimed at allowing skilled workers to fill jobs in specialized fields,

FIGURE 4.2
Citizenship and Legal Status of U.S. Immigrants: 2003

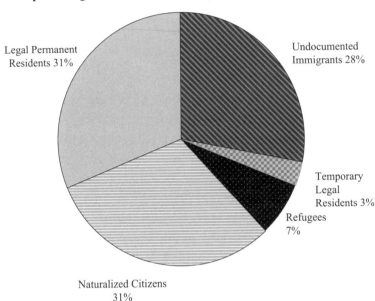

Legal Permanent Residents 31%

Undocumented Immigrants 28%

Temporary Legal Residents 3%

Refugees 7%

Naturalized Citizens 31%

Source: Urban Institute estimates based on March 2003 Current Population Survey, adjusted for undercount, and U.S. Department of Homeland Security data, as depicted in Capps, et al. (2007). Courtesy of Current Population Survey (March 2003) and U.S. Department of Homeland Security.

including computer science, engineers, doctors, college professors, nurses, and architects. However, the maximum annual limit for this group is 65,000 plus an additional 20,000 who earn a master's or higher degree in the United States. Employers initiate the process and may receive the right to hire foreign nationals under the H-1B program. These immigrants may work in the United States for up to six years. Data on the accumulated stock of these workers are not readily available, but each annual inflow is partly offset by an outflow of individuals who entered under the H-1B program and subsequently left the United States.

Immigrants will account for a substantial portion of population growth over the next 40 years. Without immigration, the U.S. population is expected to grow only modestly, at 0.45 percent per year. Such growth would be less than half of the total population growth the United States has experienced in recent decades. With expected immigration, total population growth will rise to 0.87 percent per year. Thus, immigrants are projected to account for over 50 percent of U.S. population growth.

THE GEOGRAPHY OF IMMIGRATION

Another important consideration is the geography of immigration—both in terms of the countries where immigrants are coming from, as well as the U.S. cities and states that immigrants are coming to.

As pundits and politicians are quick to point out, the faces of the foreign-born have changed. The latest wave of immigrants since the 1970s has been predominantly Asian and Latin American. Between 1970 and 2000, the percentage of foreign-born residents from Asia expanded from 8.9 percent to 26.4 percent. Latin American immigration increased even more dramatically: Latin Americans comprised 19.4 percent of the foreign-born population in 1970 and over half (51.7 percent) in 2000, as shown in Figures 4.3A and 4.3B.

Still, dramatic shifts in country of origin and race are not new in U.S. history. Another major shift occurred in the period between 1880 and 1930, when immigration from predominantly Northern European countries, such as England, France, and Germany, rapidly gave way to increased immigration from Southern and Eastern Europe. Much like Hispanic immigrants today, immigrants from Italy, Poland, and Russia brought with them new languages, cultures, and a strong sense of ethnic identity and community.

Where do immigrants settle when they arrive in the United States? The iconic image of the Statue of Liberty was indeed the first glimpse of America for millions of immigrants throughout the years. As the first federal immigration station, Ellis Island in New York harbor registered over 12 million immigrants between 1892 and 1954 (U.S. Department of the Interior 2008). Even with the closing of Ellis Island and the advent of airline travel, New York City remains the top destination for immigrants from around the world—never once relinquishing its number-one spot since the U.S. Census Bureau began keeping records in 1850. Today, 2.8 million foreign-born residents reside in the city, representing more than one-third of the population (35.6 percent; Gibson and Jung 2006, Table 23).

Although New York remains unmatched, patterns of immigrant settlement have changed dramatically in other cities around the country. Throughout the 19th century, cities on the Eastern seaboard generally held the positions as second or third most popular immigrant destinations—Philadelphia, Brooklyn (which was a separate city until 1898), Boston, and Baltimore among them. Chicago moved into second place around the turn of the century, with other Midwestern cities, notably St. Louis and Cincinnati, gaining popularity around the same time. San Francisco and New Orleans generally rounded out the top ten in the mid- to late-1800s (Gibson and Jung 2006, Table 24). California's Gold Rush of 1849 brought with it a flood of Chinese immigrants who found work in both mining and railroad construction, which, as noted earlier, later prompted the nation's first anti-immigration legislation. New Orleans, on the other hand, became a gateway for Irish, German, and Italian immigrants in this period, building on its already rich cultural heritage of French, Spanish, Creole, and Cajun residents (Hirsch and Logsdon 2008).

Today, the picture looks dramatically different. With the influx of immigrants from Latin America, it is no surprise that the city of Los Angeles now holds the number two spot. Interestingly, while the absolute number of foreign-born residents in Los Angeles is still lower than that of New York—just 1.5 million—as a percentage of the population the proportion is higher—at 41 percent. While Chicago and Philadelphia remain in the top ten, newcomers dominate, with Houston, Phoenix, San Diego, Dallas, and San Antonio making their mark as top immigrant destinations.

Where immigrants come from and where they settle are relevant to how their presence changes the economic and social life of the United States The next section focuses on the labor market consequences of immigration.

IMMIGRANTS, JOBS, AND IMPACTS ON U.S.-BORN WORKERS

The dramatic increase in immigration to the United States is surely affecting politics, economics, and culture, but many see the biggest questions as: Are immigrants taking American jobs? Did the 14 to 16 million immigrants in the 1990s who entered the country worsen job opportunities for native-born workers? Or, is the U.S. economy substantially more vibrant because immigrant workers increased capacity and the growth of several industries? Perhaps more important, how is future immigration likely to influence jobs and wages of American workers?

Although the answers are not simple, a few facts can help. Between 1970 and 2006, the percentage of foreign-born workers in the U.S. civilian labor force nearly tripled, from 5.3 to

FIGURE 4.3A
World Region of Birth of the Foreign-Born Population: 1970

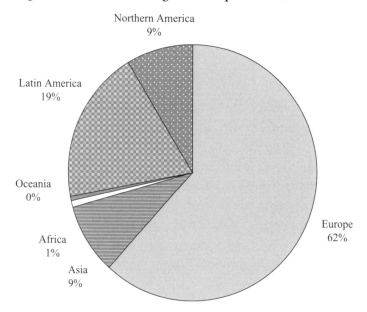

Source: Author's tabulations from Gibson and Jung (2007), Table 2.

15.6 percent. Yet, people were more able to find work in the late 1990s and early 2000s than they were in the 1970s when we had far fewer immigrants. Figure 4.4 provides dramatic evidence that rising shares of immigrants in their prime working years need not increase joblessness. Indeed, a simple reading of the graph indicates immigration reduces unemployment. Imports have not created unemployment either—imports as a share of GDP jumped from 6 percent in 1970–1971 to 16 percent in 2005–2006 while unemployment rates declined from 5.4 to 4.8 percent.

The large immigrant inflows took place in the context of a rapidly expanding labor force linked to the baby boom and the increasing job market participation of women. As the share of foreign-born 25- to 54-year-olds nearly tripled from 5.1 to

FIGURE 4.3B
World Region of Birth of the Foreign-Born Population: 2000

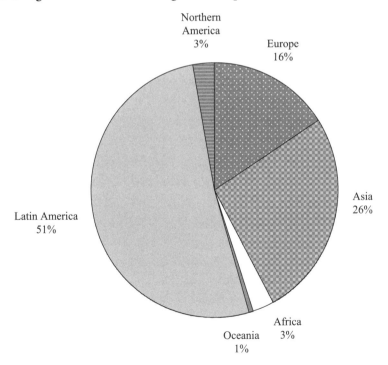

Source: Author's tabulations from Gibson and Jung (2007), Table 2.

FIGURE 4.4
Immigrant Share and U.S. Unemployment Rates: 1970–2006

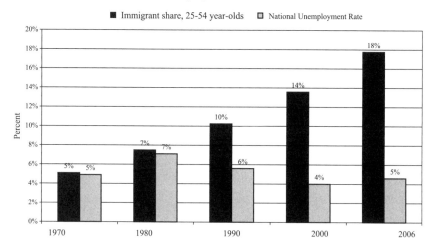

Source: For the immigrant share, see sources in Table 2.2. The unemployment rate comes from the U.S. Bureau of Labor Statistics, www.bls.gov.

13.6 percent from 1970 to 2000, the labor force jumped by about 60 million from a base of about 83 million, or 1.81 percent per year. Jobs kept pace, rising by 1.85 percent per year.

From a labor market perspective, the immigration issue is not about employment and whether legal or illegal immigrants are reducing the jobs available to American workers. The real questions are: Do inflows of immigrants reduce the wages of native workers? If so, which workers and by how much? Here, economic theory brings in three perspectives. The most straightforward is that immigrants increase the supply of labor, shifting the supply to the right in a standard supply and demand diagram. The new equilibrium should result in an increase in total employment but a reduction in wages. The increase in employment may or may not be enough to accommodate the immigrants without displacing native-born workers, but wages will generally fall. A second perspective is that inflows of immigrants expand the nation's productive capacity. If the immigrants expand the supply of each type of labor input by the same proportion and capital investment keeps pace, then the economy can expand by this same proportion without lowering overall wages, so long as aggregate demand keeps pace with our increased capacity. A third perspective is that inflows of workers of one skill group (say, unskilled workers) will complement the work of other skill groups (say, middle- and upper-skilled workers). As a result, while some workers could lose income from new competitors, others will gain from the additions to the supplies of complementary inputs.

How do the facts and research studies line up with these alternative perspectives? Let's start with the composition of immigrant workers. The most glaring educational difference between immigrant and native workers is in the share not completing high school. As of March 2007, the share without a high school education was only 6 percent among native, 25- to 54-year-old workers but nearly five times higher (28 percent) among immigrants. For immigrant workers who entered the United States in 1980 or later, the dropout proportion is over 30 percent. At the top end of the educational spectrum, immigrants hold their own. In fact, the share with a graduate degree is slightly higher among immigrants than among native-born Americans (12 percent vs. 10 percent).

Because immigrants are not distributed proportionately and instead are highly overrepresented among the least-educated workers, any negative impacts of immigrants on the workforce should surface most at the low end. Indeed, some studies (Borjas 2007) do find immigrants exerting a negative impact on wage rates that is highest among high school dropouts. Wages appear about 7 to 8 percent lower in the short run and about 4 percent lower in the long run for the dropouts. College graduates are the second most affected group, with nearly a 3.5 percent wage reduction induced by immigration. Between 2000 and 2005, Sum, Harrington, and Khatiwada (2006) point out that immigrants accounted for an astounding 86 percent of the net increase in employment, that 16- to 34-year-old men experienced a decline in employment, and that employment of young workers in a state was negatively affected by the inflow of immigrants.

Not everyone agrees about the negative impacts of immigration. Some studies examined whether the clustering of immigrants in some locations leads to lower wage rates or job opportunities relative to areas with few immigrants. One famous study looked at the impact of the Mariel boat lift of a sudden influx of Cuban immigrants into Miami (Card 1990). The expectation was that the sharp jump in immigrants would reduce job and wage opportunities in cities where immigrants settled. Yet, changes in jobs and wages in Miami were no worse soon after the influx than changes in other comparable cities. Other studies (Butcher and Card 1991; Card 2005) find low or no impacts on wages and employment in areas of high concentrations of immigrants compared to other areas. A recent study suggested immigration exerts a modest negative effect on the jobs of teenagers but not other workers, based on the differences in the concentrations of immigrants (Smith 2007). Still, the conclusion from the area-based studies is that immigration exerts a minor, if any, effect on wages and employment of native workers.

The main critique of the area studies is their failure to take account how concentrations of immigrants might push some native workers who fear losing ground to move away. If the workers affected by immigration disperse, immigration's negative impact on wages might not show up in areas of high immigrant concentration but instead would be spread over all workers in the country. Responding to this critique, Card (2005) finds an influx of high school dropout immigrants into a city substantially raises the city's share of high school dropouts, indicating that the internal migration by native dropouts does not offset the inflow of immigrants. Moreover, another market response to immigration—the influx of capital investment—should and apparently does cause all or nearly all the negative wage impacts on dropouts to go away (Ottaviano and Peri 2006; Ben-Gad 2004).

ECONOMIC EFFECTS OF IMMIGRATION ON IMMIGRANTS AND EMPLOYERS

Studies of immigration rarely examine impacts on the two groups potentially most affected—the immigrants themselves and employers. Economists and social policy advocates have bemoaned the decline in real wages of the least-educated American workers since the late 1970s. But, few, if any, have recognized that a large share of today's high school dropouts moved to the United State after 1979 (Lerman 1999). This group—which constitutes about half of prime-age male workers with less than a high school degree—generally came from very poor countries and no doubt achieved significant wage increases if we compare their wages today with what their wages were in their home countries. It is highly misleading to compare wages of today's high school dropouts with the wages of dropouts 25 to 30 years ago, because the compositions of the 1979 and 2007 dropout populations differ dramatically. In 1979, immigrants made up less than 15 percent of male dropouts (ages 25–54) in the workforce; by 2007, the immigrant share had jumped to nearly 50 percent.

Trends in real weekly earnings since 1993 illustrate the hazards of ignoring compositional factors. As Figure 4.5 reveals, the real gains for all workers are small relative to the earnings increases of both native and immigrant groups separately.[1] Put another way, one of the reasons weekly earnings appear to have stagnated for less-educated men is that this educational group is increasingly made up of immigrants. Many immigrants have weak English language skills, especially when they first enter the country. They start at wages that are very low by U.S. standards but high by the standards of their former country. Over time, immigrants achieve rapid growth in earnings—about 2.5 percent per year. In 13 years, they achieved an earnings growth of about 33 percent. If we compared their current wages to the wages they earned in their home country in 1993 or 1979, the increases would be much higher. According to one study, U.S. wages of recent immigrants in 1995 were 68

FIGURE 4.5
Earnings Per Week of High School Dropouts by Immigrant Status

■ 1993   □ 2006

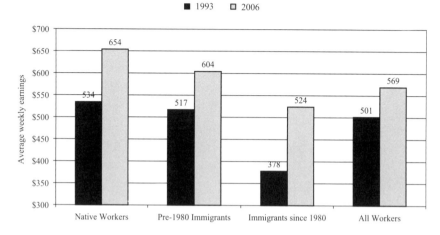

Source: Authors' tabulations of data from the March 1994 and March 2007 Current Population Surveys.

percent higher than in their last job in their home country (Jasso et al. 2000).

Some employers report that immigrants work in jobs natives are unwilling to take. Employer reports are not necessarily reliable indicators of immigration's effects on the job market since employers want to insure an adequate supply of workers without increasing wages. With fewer immigrants, some employers might have become less productive and competitive, but others might have raised wages and attracted more native workers. Immigrants taking low-skill jobs might encourage employers to move natives into more demanding positions. Indeed, recent evidence suggests that a high concentration of immigrants taking manual jobs increases demand for interactive tasks and allows natives to shift from manual to interactive work (Sparber and Peri 2007).

Certainly, some industries have increased their reliance on immigrants more than others. The most dramatic example is in construction, an industry that added 4.5 million jobs between 1994 and 2007. Immigrants who arrived after 1980 obtained over half of these jobs, raising their share of construction employment from 5 percent to 24 percent in 13 years. At the high end, immigrants obtained over 60 percent of the 450,000 increase in jobs in the computer services and computer hardware industries. However, only 29 percent of the 2.3 million new jobs in computer occupations went to recent immigrants. The temporary H1-B program no doubt contributed to availability the immigrants in computer fields.

It is hard to know how industries would have performed without the influx of immigrants. Would they have bid up wages to attract workers from other industries, would they have outsourced more work to other countries, or would their expansions have been muted? Wage patterns offer clues but no definitive answers. In the construction industry, despite a 50 percent increase in overall employment between 1994 and 2007, wages rose at a subpar 15 percent (in price-adjusted terms), well below the 24 percent real gain for all workers. On the other hand, the weekly wages in the computer industries jumped by 33 percent, as overall employment rose by 25 percent and immigrant employment by 115 percent.

DISTINCTION BETWEEN LEGAL AND ILLEGAL IMMIGRANTS

Many analyses ignore the distinction between legal and illegal immigrants, partly because standard census data sets offer no easy way of determining the legal status of immigrants. Such approaches can miss important aspects of the interaction between immigration and the job market (Smith 2006). Specialized data document that illegal immigrants have much lower education levels, are far more likely to come from Mexico, and are more recent entrants into the United States. While legal immigrants appear about as skilled as native workers, illegal immigrants have far lower educational qualifications. Thus, it is the rising share of illegal immigrants—which jumped from 5 percent in 1970 to 45 percent in 2002—and not added legal immigrants that is responsible for widening skill gap between immigrants and natives as a whole. Wage patterns mirror the less favorable job qualifications of illegal immigrants. As of 2002, legal immigrants earned nearly the same wages as natives, while the wages of illegal immigrants were 22 percent less than the wages of native workers. It is hard to know how much, if any, of the wage shortfall of illegal immigrants is linked to their lack of documentation. However, the more likely explanation is the lower educational levels and work skills of illegal immigrants.

At the other end of the spectrum are high-skill and entrepreneurial immigrants. Business leaders often point out that a striking number of immigrants have started businesses that ultimately created many jobs and even new industries. Among the major companies founded by at least one immigrant are Intel, Sun Microsystems, Google, and Yahoo. Other immigrants have started restaurants, bakeries, and specialty manufacturing companies, many of which have expanded sufficiently to create scores of new jobs. One study reported that immigrants founded 22 of the city's 100 fastest-growing companies in Los Angeles in 2005 (Miller 2007).

The United States remains open to established exceptional talent. In 2006, nearly 3,000 outstanding professors and about 9,000 multinational managers or executives obtained lawful permanent residence. Another 85,000 skilled workers with at least a BA also became permanent residents. Some of these workers were admitted on a temporary basis under the H-1B program aimed at filling selected skilled positions with temporary workers. In addition, there is a tiny program allowing individuals to become permanent residents because of their ability and willingness to invest money to create jobs, especially in targeted communities. But they number in the hundreds, averaging just over 600 people per year between 2005 and 2007.

The authorization of temporary skilled workers under the H-1B program has often been a controversial issue. Bill Gates and other well-known executives argue that it is foolish to impose restrictions on the entry of skilled workers on a temporary basis, especially in fields that they say face shortages of qualified personnel. Others argue that claims of a labor short-age are false or at least exaggerated. Even in the late 1990s, at the height of the high-tech boom, few signs of a shortage appeared in the data. For example, wage increases among computer engineers and related occupations were no higher than in other professional categories. In many cases, employers reporting that they could not find qualified personnel either paid too little or defined their qualifications so narrowly as to disqualify workers that could attain the advertised qualifications within a month or two. Recently, a National Academy of Sciences report argued that a shortfall in the number of qualified American students entering science and engineering fields is a "gathering storm" (National Academy of Sciences 2007). Yet, other evidence (Lowell and Salzman 2007) suggests the problem is too little demand for scientists and engineers—not too few young people interested in those occupations.

POLICY OPTIONS AND THE SECOND GENERATION OF IMMIGRANTS

While proponents of a literal shortage may have misstated their case, the broader questions are: should the United States base immigrant inflows on some target mix of skills? If so, what is the appropriate mix of skills? Should the current family preference policies remain in place, even if they result in an undesired skill mix? Currently, the tilt in immigration policy and immigration outcomes is strongly toward low-skill workers. Immigrant workers who entered the United States in 1980 or later only represent about 15 percent of all workers but represent 46 percent of high school dropouts. At the top end, post-1979 immigrants make up about 16 percent of those with graduate degrees. The lowest shares of immigrants are in the middle education categories (some college or an AA degree).

From one perspective, policies that encourage mainly high-skill immigration would be best for the broader economy in raising economic growth, increasing the tax base, and reducing wage inequality (Borjas 2007). The reduction in wage inequality would occur because the added competition from immigrants for high-skill jobs will lower the wage returns in those jobs relative to low-skill jobs. One possible result is that high-skill native workers lose access to high-skill jobs because high-skill immigrants accept lower wages. On the other hand, continuing to allow large numbers of less-skilled workers into the country increases competition at the low end, potentially suppressing their earnings.

Although immigration can expand the nation's productive potential, it is reasonable to ask whether certain groups should bear the entire brunt of the competition from immigrants. To maintain the immigrant contribution to overall output without concentrating the competition on selected workers, we should implement policies that encourage a balanced distribution of immigrants, one that matches the educational distribution of native-born workers. In this case, immigrants would simply add to the scale of the U.S. economy while maintaining the existing educational distribution.

What about the future? Will the U.S. economy absorb future immigrant flows into jobs without weakening the job market position of native workers? How do immigrants perform as they stay longer in the United States? Are the second and third generations of recent immigrants making progress?

In general, the outlook is promising. The growth in the U.S. workforce is slowing substantially, even with immigrant inflows at their expected levels (Toosi 2007). Between 2006 and 2016, the labor force is projected to increase by only 0.8 percent per year, well below the 1.2 to 1.3 percent annual growth over the prior two decades (1986–2006). The projected slowdown in labor force growth is especially noteworthy for prime-age work-ers. While the labor force of 25- to 54-year-olds expanded at a rapid 2 percent per year in 1986–1996, the rate of growth dropped to 0.7 percent per year in 1996–2006 and is expected to fall to 0.2 percent per year during 2006–2016. Given the slowing growth of the domestic labor force, the economy should be able to accommodate future immigrant flows more easily than in the past two decades. The continuing immigrant flows should be considered in the broader context of the globalization of services, a trend that benefits the United States in ways similar to the gains from international trade (Baily and Farell 2004). From this perspective, immigration allows employers to locate more work in the United States instead of increasing the offshoring of jobs.

Other indicators of the U.S. economy's ability to absorb immigrants effectively are the gains in earnings as immigrants stay longer in the country and the potential educational gains of the second generation. Immigrants who entered the country before 1980 earned as much as, and sometime more than, native workers. More recent immigrants, those who came between 1980 and 1992, increased their relative earnings significantly between 1993 and 2006. Note in Figure 4.6 that these immigrants averaged 80 percent of native worker weekly earnings in 2006, up from 71 percent only 13 years earlier. The gains show up for virtually every education group.

FIGURE 4.6
Weekly Earnings of Immigrants Entering the U.S. from 1980–1992 Relative To Native Workers, Age 25–54, by Education: 1993 and 2006

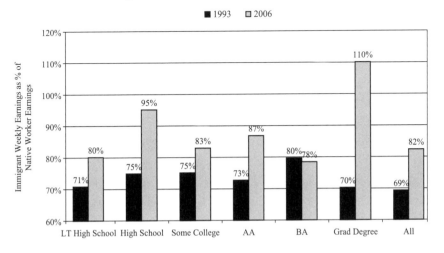

Source: See Table 4.5.

The education and skill development of the second generation will depend partly on the effectiveness of the education system as well as on the effort of immigrant families themselves. The evidence from prior cohorts—including Hispanic immigrants—suggests that children of immigrants have been achieving solid progress. While Mexican immigrants who were in their 40s in the early 1970s averaged only about 6 years of education, their children achieved twice as many years of schooling. Younger Mexican immigrants (those reaching their 40s in the late 1980s) attained an average of about 8 years of schooling and their children averaged about 12.5 years. Whether this pattern continues is an important concern.

IMPLICATIONS FOR EDUCATION

In the coming years, shifting immigration patterns will dramatically change the nature of education in the United States, but the question is: How? Will immigrant students drain resources from native-born students? Will bilingual education become the norm in elementary schools across the country? Will the children of undocumented immigrants be allowed equal access to higher education?

First, some numbers: as immigration flows have increased, both the number and proportion of school-age children of immigrants have also increased dramatically over the past several decades. The children of immigrants accounted for 19 percent or nearly one in five of all children in pre-Kindergarten to 12th grade in 2000, compared to just 6 percent of all enrollments in 1970 (Capps et al. 2005). The increase among children is actually much more dramatic than for the overall population, in part because immigrant women tend to have more children and because more immigrant women than native-born women are of child-bearing age (Capps et al. 2005). These patterns also mean that the vast majority—about three-quarters—of these 11 million children of immigrants are U.S. citizens by virtue of being born in the country. The

National Research Council predicts that if current immigration policies remain in effect and age and fertility rates of immigrants remain similar, enrollment in Kindergarten through 12th grade will increase by 21.8 million by 2050—including the children of both immigrants and native-born residents.[2] Although more moderate assumptions of intervening policies and trends lower these numbers, it is clear that the number of young people will rise if current trends continue.

What is the impact of these changes on school systems? The children of immigrants are considered to be one of the most costly consequences of immigration. Combining the burden on federal, state, and local government, the National Research Council estimates a net fiscal cost of $6,390 per capita for children of immigrants—mostly borne by state and local governments for educational expenditures. Over time, however, the report points out, these children will generate much larger positive fiscal gains as productive workers, outweighing their costs as young children and their use of social services over the lifecourse: between the ages of 20 and 64, the second generation produces a per-capita net fiscal benefit of $7,350 in tax revenue—a balance that accrues primarily to the federal government (National Research Council 1997).

While they remain in the education system, however, the children of immigrants may have more direct impacts on school spending, potentially drawing limited resources away from the children of native-born residents. Focusing on foreign-born children (rather than U.S.-born children of immigrants), a study by Schwartz and Steifel (2004) on the New York City school system, however, suggests that this is not the case for these children. At the most basic level, their data suggests that schools with higher shares of immigrant students receive less money per-pupil than schools with more native-born students—suggesting that resource allocation favors native-born students—although again, native-born students include U.S.-born children of immigrants. Further, when the authors control for individual student characteristics, they find no effect of immigrant status per se. Rather, school expenditures within the district appear to be tailored more specifically to the needs of students, such as the proportion of special education students, free-lunch eligible, and limited English proficiency—although it is important to note that foreign-born students are more likely to be limited English proficient and lower income than others.

How do immigrants fare in school? This question has garnered increasing attention in the education literature in recent years, and it is no wonder—the answer is important for several reasons. First, immigrant students may influence the achievement of their native-born peers. If, for example, immigrant students tend to be lower achieving than native-born students, they may bring down the level of instruction in the classroom or influence their peers' motivation or study habits outside the classroom. Second, as discussed earlier, the extent to which immigrants contribute productively in society is a key issue in immigration policy debates. In this context, achievement in the classroom is a key predictor of future labor market success.

The raw statistics comparing foreign-born students to their native-born peers uncovers substantially lower educational attainment and achievement for foreign-born students. A consensus in the literature reveals that foreign-born youth have consistently higher high school dropout rates and lower total years of schooling than their native-born counterparts (Fry 2007). Fry (2007) finds that among 15- to 17-year-olds, the dropout rate for foreign-born youth was almost three times that of native-born students in 2000—at 11.6 percent for foreign-born, compared to just 3.5 percent for U.S.-born. Still, Fry points out that both rates declined somewhat between 1990 and 2000 and that early childhood immigrants—those arriving in the United States before age 8—faced a dropout rate of just 5.1 percent, a rate much closer to that of their native-born peers.

The evidence on educational achievement is a bit more mixed. A recent Organisation for Economic Development and Cooperation (OECD) assessment found that foreign-born students in the

United States performed significantly worse than native-born students in mathematics and reading (OECD 2003). Others have corroborated this difference (Glick 2004, as cited in U.S. Department of Education 2007), while still others have found only insignificant differences in raw test scores and sometimes better performance for early childhood immigrants compared to native-born students (Glick and White 2003).

Many researchers argue, however, that these types of unadjusted comparisons between native and immigrant students are not appropriate. Immigrant students tend to be lower income, members of ethnic minorities, and English-language learners, suggesting that the relevant comparison should be native-born students of similar family backgrounds (Glick and Hohmann-Marriott 2007). Most studies assessing the academic achievement of immigrant students have therefore turned to multivariate analyses to control these demographic characteristics and others (for a summary of this literature, see Kao and Tienda 1995; Schwartz and Stiefel 2004).

Interestingly, virtually all of the multivariate analyses point to the conclusion that children of immigrants perform at least as well as—and often better than—children of native-born parents on measures of academic achievement. Assessing grades, standardized test scores, and college aspirations, and controlling for income and parental education, research by Kao and Tienda (1995) finds little difference between first- and second-generation children, while both groups outperform their third- or higher-generation counterparts. This pattern was especially strong among Asian students. Other studies on achievement have found similarly positive results for foreign-born students (Schwartz and Stiefel 2004), while studies of educational attainment—or number of years of schooling—have found that second-generation students attain the highest levels of education compared to their first- or third-generation counterparts (Chiswick and DebBurman 2004).

What accounts for these patterns? Economists see it as a clear case of self-selection. When compared to native-born individuals with similar backgrounds, immigrants who come to this country are likely to be highly motivated individuals—those who have a drive to create and take advantage of new opportunities for themselves and their children. Along the same lines, these immigrants may also be more hopeful about the future— a theory that educational researchers term "immigrant optimism" (Kao and Tienda 1995). Cultural values and expectations likely also play a role in the achievement of first- and second-generation students. Moreover, the positive attainment results for the second generation suggest that these students in particular may benefit from improved English language and assimilation, while at the same time benefiting from their immigrant parents' motivation or expectations.

Turning now from the children of immigrants to the immigrants themselves, what do we know about the educational attainment and English skills of immigrants? Are they indeed more likely to be less educated than native-born residents? The case is not as clearcut as it might seem. In fact, when compared to native-born residents, immigrants are clustered at both extremes of the educational spectrum. Reflecting a pattern similar to that of young adults reported earlier, the proportion of foreign-born residents that have not graduated from high school is much higher than the proportion of native-born—32 percent compared to 11 percent. At the other extreme, however, a slightly higher proportion of foreign-born individuals hold graduate degrees, as shown in Figure 4.7. This bimodal distribution of education levels is even more pronounced among recent immigrants—those who emigrated between 2000 and 2006, suggesting that this pattern will continue in the coming years.

For those at the bottom of the educational distribution, English proficiency is an important concern. A survey by the Pew Hispanic Center (Hakimzadeh and Cohn 2007), reports that among Latino immigrants without a high school diploma, only 11 percent report that they speak English very well. Not surprisingly, the percentage jumps to 62 for those with a college degree. Still, overall less than one-fourth of all first-generation Hispanic immigrants—just 23 percent—consider themselves English proficient.

FIGURE 4.7
Educational Attainment of Native-Born, Foreign-Born, and Recent Immigrants: 2006

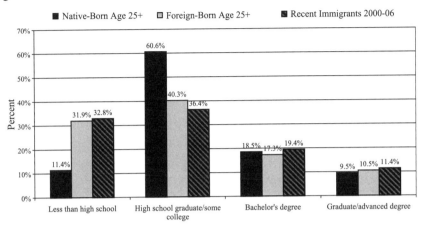

Source: Author's tabulations of Census Bureau data, 2008 Statistical Abstract, Table 42.

While many of these immigrants received schooling in their home country and continue to live and work with other Spanish-speakers after they emigrate, their children are much more proficient. Among the second generation, the percentage reporting speaking English very well jumps to 88 percent.

Certainly, the U.S. elementary and secondary education plays an important role in language acquisition among the second generation. Teachers, administrators, parents, and policymakers generally agree on the importance of developing children's English language skills, yet there is little consensus on how to achieve that goal. On one side of the debate are proponents of bilingual education, who advocate coursework in both English and the student's native language. On the other side are proponents of English-only or immersion education in which English-language-learners (ELLs) take the same courses as English speakers. Arguments for English-only education emphasize faster language acquisition when compared to bilingual education, while opponents argue that it comes at the expense of higher-level and multidisciplinary coursework, potentially lowering self-esteem, and contributing to lower overall achievement and higher dropout rates (Capps et al. 2005). While the full range of arguments for and against each approach are too numerous and controversial to address here, what is unmistakable is that after several decades of support for bilingual education throughout the 1980s and 1990s, the English-only movement has gained strength in recent years. California was the first state to move to require English-only education in 1998 with the passage of the Proposition 227 and two other states—Arizona and Massachusetts—have since passed similar legislation. The passage of No Child Left Behind will likely exacerbate this trend by placing a heavier emphasis on the speed of language acquisition. Emphasizing standardized testing (in English) and holding schools accountable for the performance of English language learners as a separate subgroup, will likely mean fewer bilingual education options in U.S. schools (Capps et al. 2005).

In contrast to the emphasis on English language acquisition among children, adult language skills have been largely ignored in policy circles. Effective communication skills are not only essential for labor market success, but they are equally important for civic engagement and daily life. A recent study by McHugh, Gelatt, and Fix (2007) on adult English-language instruction estimates that over 5.8 million legal permanent residents and 6.4 million unauthorized immigrants in the United States require adult English language instruction to raise their skills to the proficiency level needed to actively engage in civic life. Based on time-to-proficiency, they estimate that it will take a combined 596 million hours of English language instruction per year for six years to bring these two groups up to levels of proficiency necessary for passing the naturalization examination or, for younger workers, the levels of proficiency needed to enroll in postsecondary education. At an individual level, this translates to an average of 660 hours of instruction per person.

While public support for this level of instruction seems unlikely in United States, it is actually quite common in other developed countries. In Norway, immigrants between the ages of 18 and 55 are required to take a 300-hour language and social studies course, and immigrants in Germany have the option of 600, 45-minute German language courses. Australia and the United Kingdom also provide generous language instruction for adults: Australia offers between 510 and 910 hours of language instruction depending on age and refugee status, while immigrants to the United Kingdom are eligible to take English classes up to a level approximating the end of high school if they have lived in the country for a specified period of time (McHugh et al. 2007).

If young adult immigrants and the children of immigrants are able to attain adequate level of English proficiency in the United States, what are their options in postsecondary education? As U.S. citizens, the second generation born in the United States has full and equal access to the same range of educational options, including access to all public and private community colleges, vocational schools, and four-year colleges, as well as federal financial aid programs. Legal immigrants and young adults on student visas are excluded from some forms of financial aid, but otherwise face similar postsecondary options. It is undocumented immigrants and particularly the foreign-born children of these immigrants—many of whom have been educated entirely in the United States—who face the greatest challenges in obtaining postsecondary education and training.

In higher education, debates are raging over tuition policies for undocumented students. At issue is a 1996 federal law that forbade public universities from allowing undocumented students to be classified as state residents for tuition purposes. That is, undocumented students were required to pay out-of-state tuition rates. At the University of California, for example, the difference in tuition is more than $10,000—California residents pay around $7,000 in tuition and associated fees, while out-of-state tuition runs close to $18,000. Since undocumented students are currently also ineligible for federal and state financial aid programs, the 1996 law means that college education is out of reach for the vast majority of undocumented students.

In 2001, however, two states—California and Texas—passed their own laws allowing undocumented students to be classified as residents for tuition purposes. Citing the increasing social and private returns to a college education and emphasizing the inherent inequity of punishing children for the mistakes of their parents, state lawmakers attempted to circumvent the federal law. While carefully crafting the legislation to allow equal, rather than preferential, treatment of undocumented students (thereby exploiting wording in the federal law), the new laws allowed any students residing in the state for a specified period of time (one to three years) and graduating from the states' high schools to be qualified as a state resident for tuition purposes. The one catch for undocumented students was that they also must agree to pursue legalization as soon as possible.

Following the lead of Texas and California, today eight additional states have passed similar legislation—among them, Illinois, New York, New Mexico, and Kansas (Konet 2007). Each case has sparked debate and sometimes litigation over the authority of the state versus federal law. Fanning the flames, many more states have considered such legislation in recent years. In Arkansas, Governor Mike Huckabee's support of such a law played a role in his inability to secure the support of conservative voters in his 2008 bid for the Republican presidential nomination, as opponents argued that such laws were akin to amnesty (Bash 2007). In fact, to highlight their opposition, several states have gone so far as to consider or pass bills specifically denying in-state residency to undocumented students— among them, Virginia and Arizona. At the federal level, the debate continues to rage, with the so-called DREAM Act introduced several times since 2005, but never passed. Key provisions of the DREAM Act involve the repeal the 1996 law, allowing states to determine residency, and providing a pathway to citizenship for undocumented students. It remains to be seen whether the DREAM Act, or some variation of it, will pass in the years to come.

CONCLUSIONS

There is much uncertainty as to the patterns of immigration and the policies that will shape it in the years to come. As the economy slows, we may well see a natural decline in the flow of both legal and illegal immigrants. On the other hand, a new Administration and Congress may liberalize immigration, especially temporary immigration, thereby increasing the inflows of workers and their families. Over the next decades, increases in immigration will partly offset the decline in U.S. population growth. At the same time, increases in income in the primary source countries might slow the immigration rates recently experienced in the United States. Given these uncertainties and the heightened public awareness, debates over immigration policy will likely remain center stage in the political process. While there are no silver bullets for tackling the challenges of immigration, how we react to these challenges will shape the economy, our communities, and the demography of the United States for generations to come.

NOTES

1. Unless otherwise noted, the numbers cited in the next several pages come from tabulations by the authors of data from the Current Population Surveys.

2. Authors' tabulations of data from the National Research Council (1997), p. 3, and the U.S. Department of Education (2007), Table 2.

REFERENCES

Baily, Martin, and Diana Farell. 2004. "Exploding the Myths of Offshoring." *McKinsey Quarterly* Web Exclusive. http://www.mckinsey-quarterly.com/Operations/Exploding_the_myths_of_offshoring_1453.

Bash, Dana. 2007. "Rising in Polls, Huckabee Comes under Increased Scrutiny." *CNN News.* http://www.cnn.com/2007/POLITICS/12/03/huckabee.record/index.html (accessed September 15, 2008).

Ben-Gad, Michael. 2004. "The Economic Effects of Immigration—a Dynamic Analysis." *Journal of Economic Dynamics and Control* 28: 1825–45.

Bernstein, Nina. 2007. "The New Immigrant Dream: Arepas as Common as Bagels." *New York Times* (February 6), p. A01.

Borges-Méndez, Ramón, Mauricio Gastón, Michael Liu, and Paul Watanabe. 2005. "Immigrant Entrepreneurs and Neighborhood Revitalization: Studies of the Allston Village, East Boston and Fields Corner Neighborhoods in Boston." The Immigrant Learning Center, Inc. Boston: University of Massachusetts, Boston. http://site. www.umb.edu/gastonwebsite/articles/Watanabe_Entre_05.pdf.

Borjas, George. 2007. "Wage Trends Among Disadvantaged Minorities." In *Working and Poor: How Economic and Policy Changes Are Affecting Low-Income Workers*, ed. Rebecca Blank, Sheldon Danziger, and Robert Schoeni, 59–86. New York: Russell Sage Foundation.

Butcher, K. F., & Card, D. 1991. "Immigration and Wages: Evidence from the 1980s." *American Economic Review* 81(2): 292–96.

Capps, Randy, Michael Fix, Julie Murray, Jason Ost, Jeffrey S. Passel, Shinta Herwantoro. 2005. "The New Demography of America's Schools: Immigration and the No Child Left Behind Act." Washington, DC: Urban Institute Press. http://www.urban.org/UploadedPDF/311230_new_demography.pdf.

Card, David. 1990. "The Impact of the Mariel Boatlift on the Miami Labor Market." *Industrial and Labor Relations Review* 43(2): 245–57.

Card, David. 2005. "Is the New Immigration Really So Bad?" *Economic Journal* 115(507): F300–F323.

Chiswick, Barry R., and Noyna DebBurman.2004. "Educational Attainment: Analysis by Immigrant Generation." *Economics of Education Review* 23: 361–79.

Fry, Richard. 2007. "Are Immigrant Youth Faring Better in U.S. Schools?" *International Migration Review* 41(3): 579–601.

Gibson, Campbell, and Kay Jung. 2006. "Historical Census Statistics on the Foreign-born Population of the United States, 1850–2000." U.S. Census Bureau, Population Division, Working Paper No. 81. Washington, DC: U.S. Census Bureau.

Glick, Jennifer E., and Bryndl Hohmann-Marriott. 2007. "Academic Performance of Young Children in Immigrant Families: The Significance of Race, Ethnicity, and National Origins." *International Migration Review* 41(2): 371–402.

Glick, Jennifer E., and Michael J. White. 2003. "The Academic Trajectories of Immigrant Youth." *Demography* 40(4): 759–83.

Hakimzadeh, Shirin, and D'Vera Cohn. 2007. "English Usage Among Hispanics in the United States." Pew Hispanic Center. www.pewhispanic.org (accessed April 21, 2008).

Hirsch, Arnold R., and Joseph Logsdon. 2008. "The People and Culture of New Orleans." http://www.neworleansonline.com/neworleans/history/people.html (accessed April 7, 2008).

Jasso, Guillermo, Douglas Massey, Mark Rosenzweig, and James Smith. 2000. "The New Immigrant Survey Pilot (NIS-P): Overview and New Findings About U.S. Legal Immigrants at Admission." *Demography* 37(1): 127–38.

Kao, Grace, and Marta Tienda. 1995. "Optimism and Achievement: The Educational Performance of Immigrant Youth." *Social Science Quarterly* 76(1): 1–18.

Kennedy, John F. 1964. *Nation of Immigrants.* New York: Harper-Collins.

Kewal-Ramani, Angelina, Lauren Gilbertson, Mary Ann Fox, and Stephen Provasnik. 2007. "Status and Trends in the Education of Racial and Ethnic Minorities." National Center for Education Statistics, U.S. Department of Education. http://nces.ed.gov/pubsearch/pubsinfo.asp?pubid=2007039.

Konet, Dawn. 2007. *Unauthorized Youths and Higher Education: The Ongoing Debate.* Washington, DC: Migration Policy Institute.

Lerman, Robert. 1999. "U.S. Wage Inequality Trends and Recent Immigration." *American Economic Review* 89(2): 23–28.

Lowell, Lindsay, and Harold Salzman. 2007. "Into the Eye of the Storm: Assessing the Evidence on Science and Engineering Education, Quality, and Workforce Demand." Washington, DC: Urban Institute Press. http://www.urban.org/UploadedPDF/411562_Salzman_Science.pdf.

McHugh, Margie, Julia Gelatt, and Michael Fix. 2007. *Adult English Language Instruction in the United States: Determining Need and Investing Wisely.* Washington, DC: Migration Policy Institute.

Miller, Kerry. February 6, 2007. "The Impact of Immigrant Entrepreneurs." *Business Week.*

National Academy of Sciences. 2007. *Rising above the Gathering Storm: Energizing and Employing America for a Brighter Economic Future,* Committee on Science, Engineering, and Public Policy (COSEPUP). Washington, DC: National Academy Press.

National Research Council. 1997. *The New Americans: Economic, Demographic, and Fiscal Effects of Immigration.* Washington, DC: National Academy Press.

Organisation for Economic Development and Cooperation (OECD). 2003. *Where Immigrant Students Succeed: A Comparative Review of Performance and Engagement in PISA 2003.* Paris: OECD.

Ottaviano, Gianmarco, and Giovanni Peri. 2006. "Rethinking the Effects of Immigration on Wages." NBER Working Paper 12497. Cambridge, MA: National Bureau of Economic Research.

Passel, Jeffrey S. 2006. *The Size and Characteristics of the Unauthorized Migrant Population in the U.S.* Washington, DC: Pew Hispanic Center.

Passel, Jeffrey S., and Rebecca Clark. 1998. "Immigrants in New York: Their Legal Status, Incomes, and Taxes." Washington, DC: Urban Institute Press.

Schwartz, Amy Ellen, and Leanna Stiefel. 2004. "Immigrants and the Distribution of Resources Within and Urban School District." *Education Evaluation and Policy Analysis* 26(4): 303–27.

Smith, Christopher. 2007. "Dude, Where's My Job? The Impact of Immigration on the Youth Labor Market." Cambridge, MA: MIT Department of Economics.

Smith, James P. 2006. "Immigrants and the Labor Market." *Journal of Labor Economics* 24(2): 203–33.

Sparber, Chad, and Giovanni Peri. 2007. "Task Specialization, Comparative Advantages, and the Effects of Immigration on Wages." NBER Working Paper No. W13389. Cambridge, MA: National Bureau of Economic Research.

Sum, Andrew, Paul Harrington, and Ishwar Khatiwada. 2006. "The Impact of New Immigrants on Young Native-Born Workers, 2000–2005." Washington, DC: Center for Immigration Studies.

Toosi, Mitra. 2007. "Labor Force Projections to 2016: More Workers in Their Golden Age." *Monthly Labor Review* 130(11): 33–52.

U.S. Department of Education. 2007. *Digest of Education Statistics.* Washington, DC: National Center for Education Statistics. http://nces.ed.gov/Programs/digest.

U.S. Department of Homeland Security. 2007. *Yearbook of Immigration Statistics.* Washington, DC: U.S. Department of Homeland Security. http://www.dhs.gov/ximgtn/statistics/publications/yearbook.shtm.

U.S. Department of the Interior. 2008. National Park Service Web site. http://www.nps.gov/elis/historyculture/index.htm.

Five

Trends in Internal Migration

AMERICANS ON THE MOVE

One might guess that Americans today would be much more mobile than previous generations. An increase in college-going means that more young people leave home and establish new households far from their hometowns and the average American changes jobs 10.5 times in their lifetime (Bureau of Labor Statistics 2006). Add the instability in housing prices, shifts from urban to suburban living, changes in the mix of jobs across industries, and population shifts toward the Sun Belt, and one could certainly imagine that we move much more often than our parents and grandparents.

Surprisingly, this plausible image is not the reality. The Census Bureau's Current Population Survey (CPS) shows that between 2005 and 2006, only 13 percent of the U.S. population moved to another residence within the United States, compared to 20 percent between 1947 and 1948. Between these two periods, the downward trend appears to be quite steady, with a temporary surge in moves in the mid-1980s, when the decline in manufacturing employment was at its height. In any given year, U.S. residents today are less likely to move than previous generations.

But perhaps, one might guess that people today are moving longer distances, since the relative prices of travel and communication have decreased, making out-of-state moves more popular. Here again, the CPS figures do not support the claim. Of the people moving between 2005 and 2006, about 65 percent of movers stayed in the same county, almost the same share as the movers in the late 1940s (Figure 5.1) The difference in out-of-state moves is equally small—with 17 percent of all movers leaving their state today versus 16 percent in the post-World War II period.[1] While year-to-year moves across states are low as a percentage of all movers, the actual number of out-of-state moves is quite high, especially when considered over longer periods of time. Between 1995 and 2000, about 22 million people migrated from one state to another (Franklin 2003). As a result, many are not living in the states where they were born: as of 2000, 40 percent were born in a different state from where they now reside, up from about 37 percent in 1980.

While the reasons for migration are many, jobs and wages are undoubtedly the primary drivers of internal migration processes. Movement off farms to urban areas has been taking place over

FIGURE 5.1
Annual Geographic Mobility Rates, by Type of Move

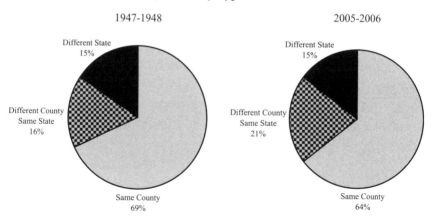

Source: Author's tabulations of data from Gibson and Jung (2007), Table A-1

the last two centuries in the United States. In 1790, rural residents made up 95 percent of the entire population. Over the next hundred years, while the urban population jumped 100 times from 200,000 to 22 million, nearly two-thirds of Americans still lived in rural areas as of 1890. The shift away from rural areas continued over the next century; by 2000, the rural population had declined to 20 percent of the United States.

Movement between regions has been less continuous. The industrialization of the Midwest and the East attracted workers from the South, especially from 1900 through 1950. With wages low in agriculture, declining world prices of cotton, the devastation of the Dust Bowl, and the migration of African-Americans, the South experienced substantial outmigration. Migration to the West began in full force after California was admitted to the Union in 1848. Since then, the population living in the Western states has continued unabated, rising inexorably from one in fifty residents in 1860 to one in four in 2000 (Yaukey, Anderson, and Lunquist 2007).

Since the 1960s, the continuing migration toward the West has been accompanied by a shift back toward the South. By the late 20th and early 21st century, even the historic movement of African-Americans from the South to the North had ended, and a reverse flow back to the South had begun. While the average annual rates of migration have varied over the last 25 years, the Northeast and Midwest have experienced steady net outmigration, while the South and West have attracted substantial amounts of net inmigration.[2] Between 1980 and 2006, the South and West attracted about 7 million and 1.4 million people, respectively, from the Northeast and Midwest. About 70 percent of the outflows came from the Northeast. International immigration largely reinforced the movement by domestic migration. Although net inmigration was positive for all regions, when counting both domestic flows and flows from abroad, the South and West attracted nearly 70 percent of all migrants.

Looking at patterns by state in Figure 5.2, we see Florida driving much of the net inflows into the South. Between 1990 and

2004, the state netted nearly 1.9 million new residents—more than double the nearly 900,000 inflow into Georgia and Arizona, the second and third most popular destinations (see Figure 5.2). Other Western and Southern Sun Belt states are pulling their weight as well, with net inflows into Nevada (which has largest inflow as a proportion to its existing population) and North Carolina rounding out the top five. As for outflows, New York State takes the cake, losing nearly 2.7 million to other states. The net outflows from California were almost as high, at 2.6 million. Illinois, Massachusetts, and New Jersey were the next highest losers in absolute terms. As the map in Figure 5.3 reveals, the state migration trends of the 1990s generally continued into the 2000–2004 period. The map illustrates the flows out of the Northeast and Midwest and toward the South and West, with some exceptions—Vermont and New Hampshire had net inflows and California and Louisiana had net outflows.

What is driving these state-level trends? Why are people moving? Jobs remain a strong motivator. Of the 13 million

FIGURE 5.2
Net Domestic Migration of Highest and Lowest States: 1990–2004

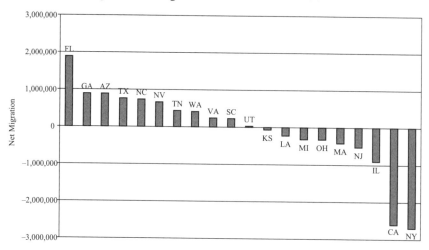

Source: Perry (2006) Table 2.

FIGURE 5.3
Internal Immigration Into and Out of U.S. States

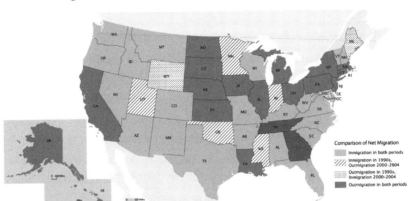

Source: Image is a reproduction of Perry (2006), Figure 3, p. 7. Courtesy of United States Census Bureau.

people moving to another county between 2005 and 2006, about one-third reported moving for employment-related reasons, including taking a new job and making the commute easier. Family-related reasons and housing-related reasons each accounted for about 26 to 27 percent of these moves.

The availability of affordable housing undoubtedly factored into many individuals' migration decisions over the past several years (Frey 2007). The Sun Belt states with the highest inflows of migrants boasted some of the most affordable housing stock in the country, with median home prices in Florida more than $14,000 below the national average (Census of Housing Web site 2008). Massachusetts, with a net outmigration, saw housing prices more than $66,000 above the national average. Whether patterns of internal migration will change substantially with the housing bust remains to be seen, but Frey (2007), reports that migration flows from high- to low-cost housing states had already slowed between 2006 and 2007.

MIGRATION TO AND FROM CITIES

Housing prices and lifestyle factors have long played central roles in another important migration trend—the suburbanization of America. The rise of urban "sprawl"—defined as in Nechyba and Walsh (2004) by lower population density and a larger city footprint—began at least as early as 1950, when the Census Bureau first began to divide urban residents in to suburban vs. center city residents (Nechyba and Walsh 2004). According to this categorization, just 35 percent of the 1950 urban population resided in the suburbs and 65 percent in the central cities, but by 1990, the percentages flipped. Over this period suburban population and land area grew steadily, while central cities have, until the last decade, largely remained stagnant on both counts. One result is a 40 percent decline in density within central cities, from about 10,000 to 6,000 persons per square mile. Meanwhile, suburban density between 1950 and 1990 declined only modestly, thus narrowing the density gap between the two urban sectors (Nechyba and Walsh 2004).

Why did people move to the suburbs? Two major economic theories offer explanations. The first is the "monocentric city model" or "natural evolution theory" in which one central business district exists within an urban area and individuals decide how far away from the central city they want to live, by comparing the cost of commuting to the price of land (see Nechyba and Walsh 2004, and Mieszkowski and Mills 1993, for detailed reviews of this literature). According to Glaeser and Kahn (2003), the growth of automobile ownership largely (pardon the pun) drove this trend, with the majority of households owning at least one car by 1952. Cars substantially cut commute times into central cities—by 1980, 84 percent of workers drove to work. A related view, espoused by Margo (1992), emphasizes the role of rising income. As income rises, economic theory suggests that families will want to buy more land and live in less densely populated areas (known as an income effect in economics)—causing many to move to the suburbs. At the same time, however, commuting becomes relatively more expensive, as each working hour is more valuable (known as a substitution effect). The choices families make will depend on which effect outweighs the other. Margo (1992) provides evidence that the income effect dominated as higher-income residents moved to the suburbs—accounting for nearly half of the growth in suburban areas between 1950 and 1980.

Although the monocentric city theory makes intuitive sense, it is limited in its focus on transportation costs. A more generally applicable and widely accepted theory of suburban growth is the Tiebout model. This model, named after Charles M. Tiebout's 1956 article, has indeed become the preferred economic model of residential mobility theory as well as a cornerstone of public economics. Tiebout suggested that people "vote with their feet," choosing where to live based on their willingness (and ability) to pay for any number of local amenities—school quality, crime rates, property taxes, and commuting distance among them. As for the growth of suburban sprawl, Tiebout's model would suggest that those who move to the suburbs sort themselves based on their preferences for lower crime, better schools, or any number of other factors, in exchange for higher commuting costs and higher tax rates.

A wealth of empirical evidence on the extent of Tiebout sorting and the influence of these various factors on internal migration has developed over the past several decades. Oates (1969) was the first to use property values to measure families' preferences for local public goods, assessing whether increased public spending on schools and other amenities raises housing prices. This work inspired a literature that looks specifically at the impact of school quality on housing prices—a discussion we return to later. Others, such as Cullen and Levitt (1999), have focused on the impact of crime on inner city population. The authors find that a 10 percent increase in crime in central cities cause the population to decline by 1 percent as people move out or refrain from moving in.

While suburban centers continue to grow, downtown areas have surged in popularity in recent years. In the 1990s, following twenty years of residential decline in central cities, the downtown population grew by a healthy 10 percent—an influx largely driven by young, well-educated, single adults. The share of 25- to 34-year-olds in downtown areas jumped from 13 percent in 1950 to 24 percent in 2000, with much of the increase coming between 1970 and 1980. The college-educated predominate in downtown areas; as of 2000, 45 percent of downtown residents had a BA or higher degree, compared to 30 percent of suburban residents and 26 percent of other city residents (Birch 2005). While the reasons for this change are still unclear, declining crime rates and urban revitalization in the 1990s undoubtedly have played significant roles in the return to central cities.

INTERNATIONAL COMPARISONS

Are Americans more mobile than residents of other countries? Although finding recent comparable data across countries is a challenge, it appears that the answer is yes. Historically, the United States has seen more mobility than most other developed countries, although Canada, Australia, and New Zealand all had similarly high percentages of population that moved over a one year period in 1970s and 1980s—at roughly 18 percent (Long 1991, as cited in Greenwood 1997). A second group of developed countries with more moderate mobility include France, Great Britain, Israel, Japan, and Sweden, with a one-year mobility rate around 10 percent. Countries with the lowest residential mobility in this period include Belgium, Ireland, and the Netherlands—around 7 percent (Long 1991, as cited in Greenwood 1997). Writing in 1976, Long and Boertlein (1976) argue that the average resident of the United States would make roughly 13 moves over his or her lifetime compared to just 8 in Britain, 7 in Japan, and 4 in Ireland (as cited in Greenwood 1997).

What drives these differences across countries? One pattern that stands out is the positive correlation between mobility and geographic size. In smaller countries, it may just be that there are fewer places to migrate, fewer options for employment in other areas, greater feasibility of commuting, or perhaps more international migration. Long and Boertlein (1976) suggest that these differences may be cultural, since the United States, Canada, and Australia consider themselves nations of immigrants in which the frontier played an important historical role. Long (1991) suggests that these countries have less restricted housing markets and a greater availability of land. These conditions foster low-cost home construction, home ownership, and movement to less-populated areas. Still, all of these hypotheses remain untested in the literature, making it difficult to isolate the factors driving international differences.

IMPLICATIONS FOR THE WORKFORCE

The willingness of workers to move toward jobs is an important component of the efficiency of the U.S. labor market. In any economy, structural unemployment can arise because of a chronic skill or area mismatch between jobs and workers. Jobs might expand in one area and stagnate in another. Without migration, unemployment might remain low in expanding areas and remain high in stagnant areas. But in the United States, as jobs migrate from one geographic area to another, workers generally follow. When unemployment rates are high in some areas and low in others, even a modest flow toward the low unemployment areas can reduce area differentials in unemployment rates. However, geographic wage differentials complicate the problem. Area differences in unemployment may persist if wages remain high in high unemployment regions. The attraction of readily available jobs may be offset by low area wage rates. Still, research indicates that increased employment opportunities in some geographic areas stimulate internal migration, which in turn generates additional economic activity and migration (Treyz, Rickman, Hunt, and Greenwood 1993).

From a theoretical perspective, individuals see migration as an investment. They experience financial and other costs today in return for a future flow of higher earnings in the destination area. As with other investments, risk and information issues can be important. High wage rates in a destination may be attractive, but the move may still be risky because of uncertainty about the quality of the job ultimately obtained and uncertainty about the possibility that competitors might migrate as well. In the United States, international immigrants might move into areas with plentiful job opportunities, thereby discouraging U.S. residents from moving into the same areas. Indeed, some researchers (Borjas 2000) have argued that metropolitan areas that attract foreign immigrants experience more outflows and fewer inflows of native workers. However, other researchers (Wright, Ellis, and Reibel 1997) find that additional foreign migrants to a metropolitan area do not discourage U.S. residents from migrating to and staying in the same metropolitan area. We discuss this issue and its implications in detail in Chapter 4.

Between 2005 and 2006, 13.7 million U.S. residents moved to another county and almost 25 million residents moved within the same county. Nearly one-third, or 4.3 million people, move for job-related reasons. This figure represents only about 3 percent of the workforce, but almost 3 times the average increase in the labor force between 2001 and 2007. Thus, annual internal migration can quickly redistribute the U.S. workforce from high to low unemployment areas. The annual flows of workers from one county to another county cumulate and in three years may reach 10 percent or more of the workforce.

In principle, internal migration is of a scale that can substantially lower the dispersion in unemployment rates across states. To illustrate, let us calculate the cumulative sum of all unemployment workers in each state in excess of 4.9 percent (approximately the average in April 2007). Put another way, how many unemployed workers in all the states with high unemployment rates would have to migrate to bring all of these state unemployment rates down to 4.9 percent? In April 2008, the figure was about 580,000. By contrast, about 1.9 million people moved from one state to another for job-related reasons. No doubt, much of the existing migration already lowered the dispersion of unemployment rates. As of April 2008, 50 percent of states had unemployment rates that fell between about 4 and 5.5 percent.

The narrow range of unemployment rates by state is especially notable in comparison to the wide dispersion of unemployment rates by region within several European countries. Within Italy, Germany, Poland, and Spain, the gap in 2003 unemployment rates between regions was about 19 percentage points, far above the U.S. differences across states or regions (Organisation for Economic Cooperation and Development [OECD] 2007). Similar differentials in the regional disparity in unemployment rates show up in comprehensive measures as well. These much higher regional differences in unemployment rates occur despite the smaller distances between regions within European countries.

In many European countries, the regional disparities in unemployment have persisted over long periods of time. Such disparities should generate incentives to move from high unemployment to low unemployment regions. But geographic mobility is far too modest to narrow the unemployment differences to low levels in these countries. Apparently, many individuals see the long run economic gain to moving as too low to justify the monetary costs, risks, or social ties lost in the process of migration. Yet, if workers do not move to the jobs, why don't the jobs move toward the workers? We would expect workers to accept lower wage rates where jobs are scarce and, in turn, the lower wage rates should attract a high demand for labor. But wages are more inflexible in European countries because wages are often set at the national level. In this case, regional differences in productivity can lead to high unemployment rates in low productivity regions. The OECD finds evidence for this relationship in many countries with high regional differentials in unemployment, indicating that the causes include a relatively immobile workforce and inflexible wages (OECD 2007). By contrast, U.S. low productivity areas are associated with low unemployment rates, suggesting that market forces operate to limit regional differences. Wages diverged in the 1980s across regions in money terms, but differences in real, price-adjusted wages continued to narrow (Eberts and Schweitzer 1994).

In addition to unemployment, internal migration can lower the variation in wage rates and in real incomes as well. *Convergence* is the common term for the narrowing of wage and income differences across areas. Standard supply and demand theory predicts convergence. Because workers are free to move within the United States, they are likely to be attracted to high wage areas and away from low-wage areas. In contrast, firms are more likely to be drawn toward low-wage areas and away from high-wage areas. The worker and firm mobility should make workers more scarce and more in demand in low wage areas and more abundant and less in demand in high wage areas. As a result, low-wage areas should experience faster wage growth than high wage areas, implying a convergence of wages and incomes.

Other theories see growth as driven by innovation that comes with high levels of human capital. In addition, skilled workers serve as complements to capital investment, increasing productivity. From this standpoint, so long as the high wages reflect high skills, high-wage areas can keep pace with or outpace low-wage areas, even allowing for the mobility of workers.

Overall, the evidence documents a considerable amount of convergence, but the narrowing is slow enough to suggest a role for the innovation-skills theory of growth. Studies reveal a high degree of convergence across states (Webber, White, and Allen 2005) and across counties (Higgins, Levy, and Young 2006). Simple comparisons show income gaps between Southern and Northern states have narrowed substantially over time. To make the comparisons concrete, consider the changing income differences between four Southern states (Alabama, Arkansas, Mississippi, and Virginia) and four Northern states (Maryland, Massachusetts, Michigan, and New Jersey). In

1929, the average income per person in the Northern states was 2.5 times the average in the Southern States. By 1950, the Northern advantage in ratio terms had declined to 1.8. In 2007, per-capita incomes in the four Northern states averaged 1.35 times per-capita incomes in the four Southern states. Overall, between 1929 and 2007, Southeast states achieved about double the rate of per-person income growth experienced by Northeast, Mideast, and the Great Lakes states. Still, some income gaps remain, partly due to the ability of some states to maintain a comparative advantage through the agglomerations of specific industries as the colocation of firms provides external benefits to neighboring firms. In addition, some of today's gap is due to price differences and does not reflect differences in real incomes.

One recent piece of research suggests that the long-term narrowing of the wage gap between the South and the North owes less to interregional mobility than to the movement of workers off the farm into nonfarm jobs (Caselli and Colemen 2001). The decline in the agricultural workforce, together with rapid increases in agricultural productivity, helped raise farm wages and returns to farmers. Since the South initially had a higher proportion of low-wage agricultural workers than the North, this shift did more to increase Southern wages. Workers had to obtain additional education and training to move into nonfarm jobs.

Within U.S. cities, the suburbanization of the population has largely gone together with the suburbanization of jobs. However, limits on the geographic mobility of some workers, especially African-Americans, can lead to unemployment and low earnings, especially among young workers (Preston and McLafferty 1999). As jobs spread more widely across metropolitan areas in the 1970s and 1980s, African-American workers experienced an increased "spatial mismatch" between workers and jobs (Stoll 2005).[3] On the other hand, whites did not see much change in the mismatch between where they live and the location of jobs (Stoll 2005). Although African-Americans have continued to live further away from jobs than do other groups, the gap narrowed over the 1990s. Jobs became more accessible to blacks, largely because they moved to more accessible homes within metropolitan areas (Raphael and Stoll 2002). Still, high levels of de facto racial segregation in metropolitan and suburban areas continue to be associated with a high level of spatial mismatch between black workers and jobs (Stoll 2005).

One way of limiting the impact of residential segregation on employment is to improve public transportation. However, in examining the impact of an extension of rail service in the San Francisco metro area, researchers found that the increased accessibility of employers increased hiring of Hispanic but not black workers (Holzer, Quigley, and Raphael 2003). More research may reveal a closer connection in the future, especially with the recent rapid rise of gasoline prices. A second way of increasing mobility is to expand access to car ownership. Raphael and Stoll (2001) estimate that racial differences in car ownership can explain a substantial share of racial differences in employment, though not everyone agrees that the finding is conclusive.[4]

Another dimension of internal migration affecting the labor market is the geographic mobility of college graduates. The rising wage gap between college graduates and high school graduates is one of the most widely recognized trends in labor economics and generally noted as a major contributor to wage inequality (Goldin and Katz 2008). Concerns over the relative decline in wages for those without a BA have contributed to important policy recommendations, including extensive subsidies for college. Yet, nearly all of the studies on this issue have relied on national data. In a recent study, Moretti (2008) takes location patterns and internal migration into account. After adjusting for differences across metropolitan areas in price levels and price trends, he finds that conventional estimates substantially overstate the current college-high school gap in real wages, as well as the change in the college wage premium. The reason is that college graduates were more concentrated and are now increasingly concentrated in metropolitan areas with high and rising living expenses, especially housing expenses. As a result, Moretti finds the real wage gap between college and high school graduates was about 40 percent in 2000, far lower than the 60 percent difference in unadjusted wages. In addition, the *increase* in the college wage premium between 1980 and 2000 is only 10 percent when wages are adjusted for differences in area price changes, well below the 20 percent using data unadjusted for these differences.

Overall, geographic mobility is substantial in the United States and contributes positively to the performance of the labor market. When jobs move, people do as well. Internal migration of workers and jobs is sufficiently large as to limit the degree of regional differences in unemployment rates to well below levels experienced in other countries.

IMPLICATIONS FOR EDUCATION

Internal migration has a particularly important influence on K-12 education for two main reasons. First, public schools are almost completely financed by state and local sources. Second, in most states and districts, a child's only public education option is the school assigned to her house.

Note first that state and local sources account for 91 percent of elementary and secondary school revenues (U.S. Department of Education 2007). Historically, the lion's share of this revenue was generated by local property taxes, making migration patterns and housing prices central to school finance debates. Since the 1970s, the relationship between local wealth and school resources has loosened, as successful lawsuits in many states led courts to mandate equitable school finance. The most famous of these was the 1971 decision in *Serrano v. Priest,* whereby California's Supreme Court ruled that the school funding system based on local property taxes was inequitable and instead required the equalization of spending per pupil across school districts. Following this landmark decision, many states followed suit by adopting similar finance equalization laws, shifting from the traditional reliance on property tax to more heavy reliance on state aid. Nationwide, state funding sources increased from 44 percent of education expenditures in 1972 to 56 percent in 2002, with per capita spending increasing by about 50 percent over the same period (Hoo, Murray, and Rueben, 2006).

Today, 44 percent of school revenue comes from local sources, and 65 percent of that funding comes directly from local property taxes (Kenyon 2007). New suburban developments add to the tax base in a local community, while declines in housing prices reduce resources available to the district. Demographic patterns also shape school resources, as older and childless families are less likely to vote to raise property taxes to support schools.

Drawing on all sources of federal, state, and local funding, public elementary and secondary school districts around the country spent on average $8,700 per student in 2006. New Jersey and New York State spent the most, at nearly $15,000 per pupil. By contrast, Utah spent only $5,464, less than 40 percent as much as the highest spending states. The Sun Belt states experiencing the greatest inflows of students from other parts of the country and from abroad, all fall into the lower half of the distribution on school spending. As Figure 5.4 reveals, the Northeastern states are generally the largest-spending districts, with the Midwestern states spending in the middle range, and the Southern and Western states at the low levels of spending.

Migration patterns may well play a role in these cost differentials, because some costs adjust only slowly. It takes time for declining districts to close schools and fire teachers and for expanding districts to build new schools and hire new teachers. As a result, we expect higher outlays per student in declining districts because they do not reduce total costs quickly in response to the declining number of students. In expanding districts, we expect crowded classrooms but lower outlays per pupil. School districts experiencing increased enrollment may

FIGURE 5.4
Current Public Spending per Pupil in Elementary and Secondary Schools by State: 2006

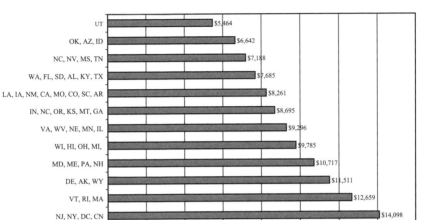

Note: States are divided into groups rounded to the nearest $500, then averaged within groups.
Source: Zhou (2008), Table 6.

benefit from expanding tax bases, but lags may slow the translation of added potential resources into more spending on schools.

Although many factors determine a state's education spending, the change in per-pupil spending might well depend on changes in enrollment. If some costs vary little with immediate changes in enrollment, the faster growth in enrollment—partly driven by internal migration—should lead to smaller increases in spending per pupil. To see whether the evidence fits, we examined the relationship between enrollment growth and spending growth across states. The results were consistent with our expectations. States with declining enrollments of 5 percent or more raised their per-pupil spending by about 29 percent in real terms, while states with expanding enrollments of 5 percent or more saw only a 21 percent increase. This relationship may understate the impacts of shifting enrollments at the school district level since the data are aggregated up to the state levels.

What about the effects of education spending on school quality? This question has sparked one of the richest literatures in academic education research. In a notable study, Hanushek (1997) reviews over 400 studies assessing the impact of school resources—including per-pupil spending, teacher qualifications, school facilities, and class size—on student achievement. The studies provide a range of answers, but he argues that on balance changes in school resources do not appear to have an independent impact on student test scores, once family characteristics are controlled for. Others, such as Card and Krueger (1996, 1998), refute this claim, finding evidence of positive effects on student achievement in studies employing the most rigorous methodology. Moreover, they argue that the evidence points to stronger effects of school resources on in the long-run—for example, on educational attainment and earnings—that may not be picked up in standardized test scores.

While the studies described earlier focus on school resources generally, a closer examination of specific types of resources can begin to answer questions as to which education investments may be most effective. For example, several notable studies using random assignment to study class size (known as the Tennessee STAR experiment), document positive effects of class-size reductions on student test scores and the on likelihood of taking college-entrance exams in high school (Krueger 1999, 2003, Kreuger and Whitmore 2001).

In an experimental setting, where we can "hold all else equal," reductions in pupil-teacher ratios may indeed be beneficial, but in reality, these reductions come at a cost. To reduce class sizes, schools may be forced to hire less-qualified teachers, potentially counteracting the gains from class size reductions. In many states, school districts can hire teachers who are not yet fully credentialed as an "emergency" measure to satisfy immediate teaching needs in response to fluctuations in enrollment. In California, for example, a district can hire uncredentialed teachers under either a waiver or an "emergency credential" if it demonstrates that it has been unable to attract fully credentialed teachers. In recent years, the proportion of uncredentialed teachers in California has climbed dramatically. In 1990–1991, only 0.4 percent of California teachers were uncredentialed, compared to 14.3 percent in 1999–1900 (Jepsen and Rivkin 2002, Table 3.2). The increase was largely in response to a 1997 act that mandated smaller class sizes, but enrollment growth from both internal and international immigration undoubtedly also played an important role.

How do uncredentialed teachers affect student achievement? The literature has overwhelmingly found that teacher "quality" matters for student performance; however, it is much less clear what types of teacher attributes and credentials constitute quality and how to measure them. Several recent studies find positive effects of teacher experience—with much of the gains coming in a teacher's first few years of teaching (Rivkin, Hanushek, and Kain 2005; Clotfelter, Ladd, and Vigdor 2007). To the extent that uncredentialed teachers have less experience than other teachers, this is likely to be an important consideration as school districts with growing enrollment seek to hire new teachers. Moreover, research by Clotfelter and colleagues (2007) estimating separate effects of state licensure on student academic performance find a positive effect of licensure, suggesting that uncredentialed teachers may indeed hinder student learning.

In addition to firing and hiring new teachers to accommodate fluctuations in student enrollment, many districts will need to consolidate or expand school infrastructure in response to population trends. Consider, for example, Clark County, Nevada, where the large number of families moving to the Las Vegas area in the 1990s led to major enrollment inflation and the construction of as many as 16 new schools in one year (Richmond 2002). Throughout the Southwest and other Sun Belt states, school openings are on the rise. In contrast, throughout the Northeast, in states like Massachusetts, and Washington, DC, school districts are facing tough (and often very political) decisions about closing schools operating below capacity. One of the most contentious examples is the District of Columbia, where 23 schools were closed in 2008 following a mayoral takeover of the school system. The closures follow years of declining enrollment in DC public schools, where enrollments have dropped by more than 60 percent over the last several decades (Turque 2008a). The closures are expected to save between $500,000 and $600,000 annually per school (Turque 2008b, 2008c)— amounting to roughly $13 million per year.

The relationship between school facilities investments and student achievement has been relatively unexplored compared to other types of school resources. In a recent paper, Cellini, Ferreira, and Rothstein (2008) find weak but suggestive evidence that investments in school facilities may cause a small increase in student test scores several years later. Perhaps more interesting, however, is that the researchers find large impacts of school infrastructure investments on housing prices. The housing price effects are too large to be explained by the effects on student achievement or by differences in the characteristics of new buyers, suggesting that parents and homeowners may value other dimensions of school outputs not reflected in test scores, such as enhanced safety, recreational opportunities, or simply the aesthetics of new school buildings.

By focusing on housing values, the Cellini, Ferreira, and Rothstein (2008) study highlights another central issue in our understanding of the implications of internal migration for the U.S. education system. Families who value education and have adequate financial resources often choose to move into good school districts—or into houses within a school district that are assigned to the best schools. This result is one of the clearest examples of Tiebout sorting. Researchers have found that parents will pay a premium of between 2 and 4 percent (Black 1999; Kane, Riegg, and Staiger 2006), for a house assigned to a school with test scores one standard deviation higher than the average school.

This type of sorting leads, of course, to schools in higher income neighborhoods becoming and remaining the "good" schools since these parents not only have more money, but are also more motivated to ensure that their children receive quality education. These parents may influence school quality directly, by volunteering at the school, getting involved in parent-teacher associations, or calling for the resignation of a poor teacher. But perhaps more importantly, they raise the quality of the school indirectly by supplementing their own child's academics by helping with homework, reading books at bedtime, fostering expectations of college-going, or passing along traits and values that helped them succeed.

One particularly troubling trend brought on by residential sorting is the resegregation of neighborhoods and schools along racial and socioeconomic lines. The famous 1955 Supreme Court decision in *Brown vs. Board of Education* made racially segregated schooling illegal, but with homes closely tied to school assignments, the next half-century witnessed "white-flight" in many parts of the country, as affluent white families moved out of urban school districts to the suburbs.

The result has been continued disparities both in school inputs and student outcomes in along racial and socioeconomic lines. Although some progress has been made in equalizing school finance (e.g. with the *Serrano v. Priest* decision, noted earlier), to the extent that districts still draw on local property taxes, districts with lower-income students are much more likely to suffer from outdated facilities, overcrowding, and other problems with physical facilities. For example, 43 percent of schools serving the poorest students rely on temporary or portable classrooms, compared to 27 percent among the richest schools (U.S. Department of Education 2007, Table 98). Even within districts, resources may be inequitably distributed, as highly qualified teachers gravitate to schools with higher-achieving students, while novice and emergency credentialed teachers are matched to schools with disadvantaged students (Lankford, Loeb, and Wyckoff 2002; Hanushek, Kain, and Rivkin 2004; Reed, Rueben, and Barbour 2006; Clotfelter, Ladd, and Vigdor 2005).

Whether it is the resources themselves or the numerous other factors that drive student achievement, sizable differences between the test score of black and white students remain. In 2004, 78 percent of nine-year-old white students met basic proficiency in reading on the National Assessment on Educational Progress (NAEP) exam, compared to just 51 percent of black students.[5] Educational attainment is also markedly different across racial and ethnic lines. Among 16- to 24-year-olds, the dropout rate for blacks is 10.7 percent and for Hispanics it is 22.1 percent, compared to just 5.8 percent for whites (U.S. Department of Education 2007, Table 105).

What can be done? While space does not permit in-depth discussion of the many policy options, one particular option is especially relevant to internal migration, since it has the potential to influence residential location patterns in the United States—that policy is school choice. School choice policies can take a range of forms, including voucher programs, in which students receive money to attend the private school of their choice, and charter school programs, which allow entrepreneurs to create new schools with public funds. But perhaps the simplest school choice program is one in which students simply have a choice of attending any public school in the district. Charlotte, North Carolina, recently implemented such a program. Students were assigned a "home" school, but were allowed to submit an application to attend up to three other public schools in the district. The key concept is that choice uncouples school assignments from housing decisions, potentially resulting in greater neighborhood and school integration as well as a more equal distribution of housing prices within districts.

Up to now, we have focused on K-12 education, but migration patterns also have important implications for higher education. While enrollments in postsecondary education will likely continue to increase in the United States as a whole, states with net outmigration may see decreased demand for local colleges. In fact, many Northeastern and Midwestern colleges are anticipating declining applications as early as 2009 and are expanding recruiting efforts in the growing Sun Belt states (Strauss 2008).

It's not just colleges that are feeling the pressure of migration and demography. State policymakers and employers are increasingly concerned about the outmigration of talented college students. Compared to previous generations, students today are much more likely to move to attend a four-year college in another state. Hoxby (1997) reports that in 1994, 25 percent of four-year college students attended a college or university outside their home state compared to just 7 percent in 1949. Hoxby argues that before the 1950s students predominately attended colleges and universities close to home, resulting in a collection of small, autonomous, often monopolistic, local markets for college education (Hoxby 1997). Between the 1940s and 1970s, however, several important changes took place that increased competition between schools and students on a national scale. Not least among these changes was a sharp decline in the cost of travel and communications that came along with deregulation of the airline and telecommunication industries in the 1970s (Hoxby 1997).

Today, with unlimited nationwide long distance cell phone plans (not to mention unlimited text messaging) and a vast array of low-cost airlines to choose from, students have even fewer constraints preventing them from leaving home for their college education. Yet, surprisingly, out-of-state college-going has not changed substantially in the years since Hoxby's study. The Digest of Education Statistics reports that, as in Hoxby's 1994 figures, 74 percent of four-year college freshmen who graduated high school in the previous year attended college in their home state in 2004 (U.S. Department of Education 2006, Table 209). It may be that the forces of lower-cost communication and travel have been counteracted by rising housing costs—providing an increased incentive to live at home. Adding to this effect may be the rising cost of out-of-state college tuition and the growing availability of community college options across the country.

More striking than these patterns of college-going, however, are comparisons across states. Figure 5.5A shows the ten states with the highest and lowest percentages of students staying in state, while Figure 5.5B shows the states with the highest and lowest net in- and outmigration of college freshmen. The District of Columbia has the lowest in-state percentage at just 7 percent. Texas is at the top of the list with 92 percent staying in-state, with California a close second at 90 percent. In absolute numbers, however, California and Texas see more net outmigration than most other states—that is, the roughly 8 to 10 percent of students that migrate out of these extremely populous states outnumber the high proportion of leavers in small states. Nonetheless, some small states see large net inmigration: over 20,000 freshmen moved to New Jersey to attend college in 2004.

FIGURE 5.5A
Highest and Lowest Percentage of In-State Freshmen, Fall 2004

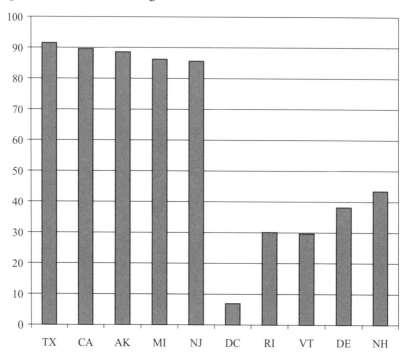

Source: Author's tabulations of data from U.S. Department of Education, National Center for Education Statistics, Digest of Education Statistics: 2006, Table 209.

FIGURE 5.5B
Highest and Lowest Net Migration of Freshmen, Fall 2004

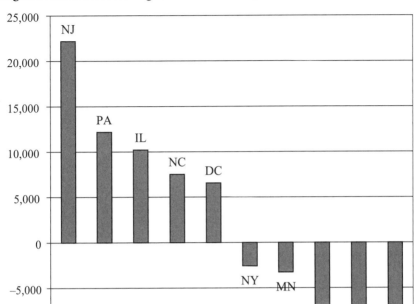

Source: Author's tabulations of data from U.S. Department of Education, National Center for Education Statistics, Digest of Education Statistics: 2006, Table 209.

What accounts for these astounding differences across states? Why do some states see a "brain drain" and others a "brain gain"? As is the case for internal migration generally, geography is, again, an important factor. The distance to another state is much smaller in smaller states—reducing travel costs for out-of-state students and making it more likely that a student will travel out of state for their education. Another obvious driving force is the quality and variety of college options available to state residents. Smaller states, like Vermont and Rhode Island, tend to have fewer options and often only one flagship public institution. In California, the University of California and California State Universities, together boast 33 campuses across the state. The extent to which a state invests in its public education system—and the competitiveness of those public institutions on a national scale—undoubtedly influences the extent of brain gain or drain in the state.

In recent years, several states have implemented policies designed specifically to slow brain drain or promote brain gain, and no policy has proven more popular than state merit-based financial aid programs. The state of Georgia was the first to implement such a program in 1993, offering all high school graduates with a 'B' average a scholarship covering tuition, fees, and books at one of Georgia's public colleges. Alternatively, students could opt instead to receive the equivalent value to defray some of the costs of a private college education, as long as that college was located in the state. Was the policy successful at stopping the brain drain? Research by Corwell, Mustard, and Sridhar (2006) suggests that it was. The authors find that the scholarship reduced the number of college students leaving the state by 560 students per year.

Following Georgia's lead, at least 13 other states across the United States have implemented similar programs including Florida, New Mexico, Alaska, Michigan, and more recently Tennessee and Massachusetts (Heller 2004). Despite their apparent effectiveness at reducing brain drain, however, these programs raise serious questions of equity and efficiency. Numerous studies have shown that merit-based scholarships disproportionately serve students who would have attended college even without the subsidy—most often affluent white students. These types of scholarships do little to open access to education or increase college-going among underserved groups (for a review of this literature and several studies along these lines, see Heller and Marin 2004). Faced with tight budgets and skyrocketing tuition, states have to weigh their effort to retain top students against the need for their scarce resources to go to the low-income students who need it most. Replacing merit-based programs with additional funding for need-based programs would go far toward reducing inequality of access. In addition, by expanding college access to those who would otherwise not attend, need-based aid can raise the overall level of human capital in the state.

CONCLUSIONS

Americans have long been geographically mobile. Over the last two centuries, Americans have shifted from rural to urban-suburban areas and from the East and Midwest to the West. Recently, the South has experienced a resurgence in population. But, while Americans move often, internal migration has been gradually declining since the late 1940s.

Patterns of internal migration are both a cause and consequence of changing economic, social, and policy conditions. In the case of the job market, migration is largely a response to the differences in the availability of opportunities. High unemployment pushes some people to relocate to areas with more jobs; job transfers within a company cause some to move across geographic boundaries. Even modest levels of mobility are able to help the United States achieve relatively low regional disparities in unemployment. Geographic mobility can play a role in affecting wage differences as well, as workers move from low- to high-wage areas and cause real wages to converge. For determining how area wage differences translate into area differences in living standards, one must use data that accounts for price differences as well. A recent paper finds that shifts in the location of college graduates toward high-cost metropolitan areas help explain a substantial share of the college-high school gap in wages and trends in this gap.

In the case of education, migration is less a response than a cause of challenges for schools systems. Moves away from central cities to the suburbs have reduced the number of students in urban school systems and led to increases in the share of minority students. Interstate migration has required cutbacks in schooling many states and expansions in other states.

What about the future? Certainly, people will continue to move to find improved housing, start families, and take new jobs, but recent trends suggest a decline in overall residential movement and migration between counties. Some of the reduction in mobility between 1988 and 2006 reduction in mobility is due to the rise in homeownership, but most involves the decline in moves by both renters and owners. The impact of the 2007–2008 decline in house prices is uncertain. It might increase residential movement, as lower prices in some areas attract new buyers and because the increase in rental-occupied units raises mobility since renters move more than homeowners. Alternatively, it might reduce movement as potential sellers choose to stay in their homes instead of selling at what they see as depressed prices. Finally, the return to cities and the slow-down in house prices in selected areas indicate that the broad trends toward suburbanization and migration to the "Sun Belt" states are moderating.

NOTES

1. Information from CPS annual mobility tables, http://www.census.gov/population/socdemo/migration/tab-a-1.pdf.

2. The data are based on tabulations from Table A-2. Annual Inmigration, Outmigration, Net Migration, and Movers from Abroad for Regions: 1980–2006, U.S. Bureau of the Census. See http://www.census.gov/population/socdemo/migration/tab-a-2.pdf.

3. John Kain (1968) first estimated the impact of residential segregation on the jobs of blacks. Since then, a variety of researchers have attempted to assess the impact of spatial mismatch on jobholding among disadvantaged groups. See Preston and McLafferty (1999) for a brief review of the John Kain's spatial mismatch theory.

4. See, for example, the comment by Clifford Winston (2001).

5. Here, we define proficiency as achieving a score of 200 out of 500 on the NAEP reading exam. According to the Digest of Education Statistics (2007) "Students scoring 200 are able to understand, combine ideas, and make inferences based on short uncomplicated passages about specific or sequentially related information" (Table 115).

REFERENCES

Birch, Eugenie L. 2005. *Who Lives Downtown*. Brookings Institution, Metropolitan Policy Program, Living Cities Census Series. Washington, DC: Brookings Institution.

Black, Sandra E. 1999. "Do Better School Matter? Parental Valuation of Elementary Education." *Quarterly Journal of Economics* 114(2): 577–99.

Borjas, George. 2000. "Economics of Migration." For *International Encyclopedia of the Social and Behavioral Sciences.* Section No. 3.4, Article No. 38.

Bureau of Labor Statistics. 2006. "National Longitudinal Survey of Youth, 1979." http://www.bls.gov/news.release/pdf/nlsoy.pdf (accessed May 30, 2008).

Card, David, and Alan Krueger. 1996. "School Resources and Student Outcomes: An Overview of the Literature and New Evidence from North and South Carolina." *Journal of Economic Perspectives* 10(4): 31–50.

Card, David, and Alan Krueger. 1998. "School Resources and Student Outcomes." *Annals of the American Academy of Political and Social Science* 559: 39–53.

Caselli, Francesco, and Wilbur Colemen II. 2001. "The U.S. Structural Transformation and Regional Convergence: A Reinterpretation." *Journal of Political Economy* 109(3): 584–616.

Cellini, Stephanie Riegg, Fernando Ferreira, and Jesse Rothstein. 2008. "The Value of School Facilities: Evidence from a Dynamic Regression Discontinuity Design." NBER Working Paper No. 14516, Cambridge, MA: National Bureau of Economic Research.

Clotfelter, Charles T., Helen F. Ladd, and Jacob L. Vigdor. 2005. "Who Teaches Whom? Race and the Distribution of Novice Teachers." *Economics of Education Review* 24: 377–92.

Clotfelter, Charles T., Helen F. Ladd, and Jacob L. Vigdor. 2007. "How and Why Do Teacher Credentials Matter for Student Achievement?" National Bureau of Economic Research (NBER) Working Paper No. 12828, Cambridge, MA: National Bureau of Economic Research.

Cornwell, Christopher, David B. Mustard, and Deepa J. Sridhar. 2006. "The Enrollment Effects of Merit-Based Aid: Evidence from Georgia's HOPE Scholarship." *Journal of Labor Economics* 24(4): 761–86.

Cullen, Julie, and Steven Levitt. 1999. "Crime, Urban Flight, and the Consequences for Cities." *Review of Economics and Statistics* 81(2): 159–69.

Eberts, Randall, and Mark Schweitzer. 1994. "Regional Wage Convergence and Divergence: Adjusting Wages for Cost of Living Differences." *Economic Review* 30(3): 26–37.

Franklin, Rachel. 2003. "Domestic Migration across Regions, Divisions, and States, 1995–2000." Washington, DC: U.S. Bureau of the Census.

Frey, William H. 2007. "Housing Bust Shatters State Migration Patterns." Washington, DC: Brookings Institution. http://www.brookings.edu/opinions/2007/~/media/Files/rc/opinions/2007/1228_migration_frey/1228_migration_frey.pdf.

Glaeser, Edward, and Matthew Kahn. 2003. "Sprawl and Urban Growth." NBER Working Paper No. 9733. Cambridge, MA: National Bureau of Economic Research.

Goldin, Claudia, and Lawrence Katz. 2008. *The Race between Education and Technology.* Cambridge, MA: Belknap Press of Harvard University Press.

Greenwood, Michael J. 1997. "Internal Migration in Developed Countries." Ch. 12 of *Handbook of Population and Family Economics*, ed. M. R. Rozenzwieg and O. Stark. Amsterdam: Elsevier Science.

Hanushek, Eric A. 1997. "Assessing the Effects of School Resources on Student Performance: An Update." *Education Evaluation and Policy Analysis* 19(2): 141–64.

Hanushek, Eric A., John F. Kain, and Steven G. Rivkin. 2004. "Why Public Schools Lose Teachers." *Journal of Human Resources* 39(2): 326–54.

Heller, Donald E. 2004. Chapter 1 of *State Merit Scholarship Programs and Inequality*, ed. D. E. Heller and P. Marin. Cambridge, MA: Civil Rights Project at Harvard University.

Heller, Donald E., and Patricia Marin (Eds.). 2004. *State Merit Scholarship Programs and Inequality.* Cambridge, MA: Civil Rights Project at Harvard University.

Higgins, Matthew J., Daniel Levy, and Andrew T. Young. 2006. "Growth and Convergence across the United States: Evidence from County-Level Data." *Review of Economics and Statistics* 88(4): 671–81.

Holzer, Harry, John M. Quigley, and Steven Raphael. 2003. "Public Transit and the Spatial Distribution of Minority Employment:

Evidence from a Natural Experiment." *Journal of Policy Analysis and Management* 22(3): 415.

Hoo, Sonya, Sheila Murray, and Kim Rueben. 2006. "Tax Facts: Education Spending and Changing Revenue Sources." Tax Policy Center at Urban Institute and the Brookings Institution (April 10). http://www.urban.org/url.cfm?ID=1000942 (accessed May 27, 2008).

Hoxby, Caroline M. 1997. "How the Changing Market Structure of U.S. Higher Education Explains College Tuition." NBER Working Paper No. 6323. Cambridge, MA: National Bureau of Economic Research.

Jepsen, Christopher, and Steve Rivkin. 2002. "Class Size Reduction, Teacher Quality, and Academic Achievement in California Public Elementary Schools." Public Policy Institute of California. http://www.ppic.org/content/pubs/report/R_602CJR.pdf.

Kain, John. 1968. "Housing Segregation, Negro Employment, and Metropolitan Decentralization." *Quarterly Journal of Economics* 83: 175–97.

Kane, Thomas J., Stephanie K. Riegg, and Douglas O. Staiger. 2006. "School Quality, Neighborhoods, and Housing Prices." *American Law and Economics Review* 8(2): 183–212.

Kenyon, Daphne A. 2007. *The Property Tax–School Funding Dilemma.* Policy Focus Report. Cambridge, MA: Lincoln Institute of Land Policy.

Krueger, Alan. B. 1999. "Experimental Estimates of Education Production Functions." *Quarterly Journal of Economics* 114(2): 497–532.

Krueger, Alan B. 2003. "Economic Considerations and Class Size." *Economic Journal* 113: F34–F63.

Krueger, Alan B., and Diane M. Whitmore. 2001. "The Effect of Attending a Small Class in the Early Grades on College Test-Taking and Middle School Test Results: Evidence from Project STAR." *Economic Journal* 113: 1–28.

Lankford, Hamilton, Susanna Loeb, and James Wyckoff. 2002. "Teacher Sorting and the Plight of Urban Schools: A Descriptive Analysis." *Educational Evaluation and Policy Analysis* 24: 37–62.

Long, L. H. 1991. "Residential Mobility Differences Among Developed Countries." *International Regional Science Review* 14: 133–47.

Long, L. H. and C. G. Boertlein. 1976. "The Geographic Mobility of Americans: An International Comparison." Current Population

Reports, Special Studies, Series P-23, No. 64. Washington, DC: U.S. Bureau of the Census.

Margo, Robert. 1992. "Explaining the Postwar Suburbanization of Population in the United States: The Role of Income." *Journal of Urban Economics* 31(2): 310.

Mieszkowski, Peter, and Edwin S. Mills. 1993. "Causes of Metropolitan Suburbanization." *Journal of Economic Perspectives* 7(3): 135–47.

Moretti, Enrico. 2008. "Real Wage Inequality." National Bureau of Economic Research (NBER). Working Paper No. 14370. Cambridge, MA: National Bureau of Economic Research.

Nechbyba, Thomas J., and Randall P. Walsh. 2004. "Urban Sprawl." *Journal of Economic Perspectives,* 18(4): 177–200.

Oates, Wallace. 1969. "The Effects of Property Taxation and Local Spending on Property Values: An Empirical Study of Tax Capitalization and the Tiebout Hypothesis." *Journal of Political Economy* 77: 957–71.

Organisation for Economic Development. 2007. *Regions at a Glance, 2007.* Paris: OECD.

Perry, Marc. 2006. *Domestic Net Migration in the United States.* Current Population Reports. P25-1135. Washington, DC: U.S. Bureau of the Census.

Preston, Valerie, and Sara McLafferty. 1999. "Spatial Mismatch Research in the 1990s: Progress and Potential." *Papers in Regional Science* 78(4): 387–402.

Raphael, Steven, and Michael A. Stoll. 2001. "Can Boosting Minority Car Ownership Rates Narrow Inter-Racial Employment Gaps?" *Brookings-Wharton Papers on Urban Affairs* 2: 99–137.

Raphael, Steven, and Michael A. Stoll. 2002. "Modest Progress: The Narrowing Spatial Mismatch between Blacks and Jobs in the 1990s." Washington, DC: Brookings Institution.

Reed, Deborah, Kim S. Rueben, and Elisa Barbour. 2006. "Retention of New Teachers in California." Public Policy Institute of California. www.ppic.org/content/pubs/R_206DRR.pdf (accessed June 10).

Richmond, Emily. March 6, 2002. "Class Size Threatens School Accreditation." *Las Vegas Sun.* http://www.lasvegassun.com/news/2002/mar/06/class-size-threatens-school-accreditation.

Rivkin, Steven G., Eric A. Hanushek, and John F. Kain. 2005. "Teachers, Schools and Academic Achievement." *Econometrica* 79: 418–58.

Stoll, Michael. 2005. "Geographic Job Skills Mismatch, Job Search, and Race." *Urban Studies* 42(4): 695–717.

Strauss, Valerie. 2008. "Population Shift Sends Universities Scrambling." *Washington Post* (March 10), p. A01.

Taylor, Jim, and Steve Bradley. 1997. "Unemployment in Europe: A Comparative Analysis of Regional Disparities in Germany, Italy, and the UK." *Kyklos* 50(2): 221–45.

Tiebout, Charles M. 1956. "A Pure Theory of Local Expenditure." *Journal of Political Economy* 64: 416–24.

Treyz, George I., Dan S. Rickman, Gary L. Hunt, and Michael J. Greenwood. 1993. "The Dynamics of U.S. Internal Migration." *Review of Economics and Statistics* 75(2): 209–14.

Turque, Bill. 2008a. "Study Highlights Change in DC School Enrollment." *Washington Post* (April 25).

Turque, Bill. 2008b. "Rhee's Need to Hurry Runs Into Parents' Fear of Change" *Washington Post* (May 7).

Turque, Bill. 2008c. "Conflicting Feelings as Elementary School Marks Its End." *Washington Post* (June 1).

U.S. Census Bureau. 2008. Census of Housing Web site. http://www.census.gov/hhes/www/housing/census/historic/values.html (accessed April 23, 2008).

U.S. Department of Education. 2007. *Digest of Education Statistics.* Washington, DC: National Center for Education Statistics. http://nces.ed.gov/Programs/digest.

U.S. Department of Education. 2006. *Digest of Education Statistics.* Washington, DC: National Center for Education Statistics, http://nces.ed.gov/Programs/digest.

U.S. Department of Education. 2007. *Digest of Education Statistics.* Washington, DC: National Center for Education Statistics. http://nces.ed.gov/Programs/digest.

U.S. Department of Education. 2008. Education Finance Statistics Center Web site (Edfin). http://nces.ed.gov/edfin.

Webber, Don, Paul White, and David O. Allen. 2005. "Income Convergence across U.S. States: An Analysis Using Measures of Concordance and Discordance." *Journal of Regional Science* 45(3): 565–89.

Winston, Clifford. 2001. "Comment." *Brookings-Wharton Papers on Urban Affairs* 2: 140–42.

Wright, Richard A., Mark Ellis, and Michael Reibel. 1997. "The Linkage Between Immigration and Internal Migration in Large Metropolitan Areas in the United States." *Economic Geography* 73(2): 234–54.

Yaukey, David, Douglas Anderson, and Jennifer Hicks Lundquist. 2007. *Demography: The Study of Human Populations.* Long Grove, IL: Waveland Press.

Zhou, L. (2008). *Revenues and Expenditures for Public Elementary and Secondary Education, School Year 2005–2006 (Fiscal Year 2006)* (NCES 2008-328). National Center for Education Statistics. Institute of Education Sciences. Washington, DC: U.S. Department of Education. http://nces.ed.gov/pubsearch/pubsinfo. asp?pubid=2008328.

Six

Summing Up

The 20th century witnessed nearly a fourfold increase in the U.S. population, together with dramatic shifts in where people come from, where they live, and how they combine into households. Having reviewed the aging of the U.S. population, striking shifts in the U.S. family and household structure, and the dynamic patterns of internal migration and international immigration, we now ask—how do these individual components add up to shape the future population of the United States? How are the trends likely to interact? Are the interactions likely to intensify or to modify our conclusions about demographic impacts on the labor market and educational system?

Previous chapters have highlighted several trends that will alter the future demography of the United States. The best known are the aging of the population and the increasing shares of children living away from both parents. Although immigration as a public issue usually relates to illegal immigration, we have emphasized the ups and downs in overall immigration, but we take note of the increasing shares of immigrants, both legal and illegal, from Latin America. We further find high levels of mobility within the United States and particularly high population growth rates in the South and West relative to rates in the Northeast and Midwest. This chapter looks beyond these individual demographic components to consider the interactions across components and their implications for labor markets and the educational system.

We are not so bold as to forecast the demography of the entire 21st century, but existing patterns and trends can yield plausible projections of the U.S. population over the next few decades. One reason is that most of the population of 2030 already is alive and residing in the United States Although there are uncertainties associated with immigration, internal migration, life expectancy, marriage and divorce, and child rearing, the next decades are unlikely to generate change as demographically eventful as the 20th century or even the last 60 years. Still, an important caveat about these projections is the considerable uncertainty about the levels and composition of immigration, in particular. The methods used to project immigration rely heavily on past trends along with the recognition that short-term immigration levels generally depend on job growth in the United States. The analyses generally take little or no account of the impact on immigration from public policies or from economic development in source countries.[1]

AGING AND IMMIGRATION

With declines in birth rates and longer life expectancies of adults, the share of the population over age 65 will jump from about 12 percent in 2000 to 20 percent in 2030. While this trend contributes to stagnant population levels in other developed countries, in the United States, population growth will continue at a healthy pace through 2030. In fact, the growth of the U.S. population is projected at about 9 percent per decade, not far below earlier decades.

The reason for this pattern is the interaction between population aging and immigration. The combination of legal and undocumented immigrants is expected to account for nearly half the U.S. population growth through 2030; in contrast, the immigrant share of growth was about 30 percent between 1980 and 2000. While the native-born population of 25- to 54-year-olds will experience no growth at all in the next three decades, continuing high levels of immigration will more than offset this shortfall. Hispanics in this age group will increase by 45 percent, with over half of the increase associated with immigration. In the case of Asian-Americans, immigration will account for all of its expected 39 percent growth.[2]

Patterns of population aging by race and ethnicity are notable. The white, non-Hispanic population is aging most rapidly; its over-65 population is projected to rise from 14 percent of the total in 2000 to 25 percent in 2030. Although aging will take place among other race and ethnic groups, these groups start from a much lower base. For example, only 5 percent of all Hispanics are over age 65 today; by 2030, the Hispanic elderly share is projected at 10 percent. Population aging will also take place among blacks and Asian-Americans as well, but like Hispanics, their proportions of elderly will remain relatively low compared to non-Hispanic whites. As racial and ethnic minorities become an increasing proportion of the population, their lower shares of elderly will limit the extent of population aging in the United States.

Meanwhile, the population of children (0- to 19-year-olds) is projected to grow at about 0.7 percent per year, well above the 0.4 percent growth rate for 25- to 54-year-olds. Trends by race and ethnicity will be similar for the two age groups. In line with low birth rates and population aging, the number of non-Hispanic white children will decline by 2 million. But, these losses will again be more than offset by increases in the children of other groups, particularly Hispanics. By 2030, Hispanic children will comprise 31 percent of all 0- to 19-year-olds, a pattern we discuss further in the next section.

IMMIGRATION AND INTERNAL MIGRATION

Another aspect of immigration is geographic composition. In Chapter 4, we noted that while California and New York remain the top two states in terms of the immigrant share of the population, recent immigrant penetration has become somewhat more disbursed. Four states (California, New York, Texas, and Florida) accounted for 63 percent of the U.S. foreign-born population, but only about half of the 1990–2007 increase in the foreign-born population.[3] The influx of immigrants over this period partly has offset internal outmigration and slower population growth in California and New York, but has partly reinforced internal inmigration and rapid growth in Florida and Texas. In the absence of a rising number of immigrants, New York and New Jersey would have experienced virtually no population growth instead of 7 percent and 12 percent, respectively.[4]

One possibility is that the immigration aiding slow growth states is temporary and that subsequent generations, especially the more highly educated immigrants, will move to fast-growing states. The evidence suggests otherwise. Although immigrants who were very young when they came to the United States move somewhat more frequently than the native-born, the moves are generally toward states with already high concentrations of immigrants (Ellis and Goodwin-White 2006). Still, the impacts of additional immigrants on the state shares of the population are modest, even in the high immigration states. The 2007 populations of California, New York, New Jersey, Texas, and Florida would have been 34.2 percent without immigration, instead of the actual 35.4 percent.

IMMIGRATION AND FAMILY STRUCTURE

Another interaction is between immigration and family structure. Immigration and differences in birth rates will alter the race and ethnic composition of children, but this change looks to have little impact on whether children are living in a two-parent family. About 70 percent of American children lived in a two-parent family in 2008. Non-Hispanic white children are more likely to live with two parents than the average child (79 percent vs. 70 percent) and are declining in numbers. However, the two ethnic groups expanding their shares of children have rates near the national average (Hispanics at about 67 percent) or above the average (Asians at 83 percent).

Moreover, projections about the influence of race and ethnic composition on family structure are complicated by intermarriage and the assimilation of future generations. Much of the rise in the Hispanic population will be among the second and third generation of immigrants. These groups intermarry with non-Hispanics at medium to high rates—33 among second generation Hispanics and 57 percent among third generation Hispanics (Suro and Passell 2003).

INTERNAL MIGRATION AND AGING

These two trends may interact if the increasing share of older people leads to higher rates of internal migration, as retirees move from the Northeast and Midwest to the southern and western parts of the United States. In fact, older individuals are less likely to move than younger people. Only about 22 percent of those 65 and older move at all, and less than 20 percent of these movers migrate to another state (He and Schachter 2003). Thus, only about 4 percent of the 65 and over population moves out of state over a five-year period. Perhaps not surprisingly, the two states with the largest net inflows of older people between 1995 and 2000 were Florida and Arizona, while New York and Illinois saw the largest net outflows of people in this age group.

Internal migration to some states will reinforce already high population growth, while in other states slow growth linked to population aging will decline further because of outmigration. The United States as a whole will see about a 25 percent rise in population between 2000 and 2030 alongside an increase from 12.7 to 19.7 in the 65 and over share of the population. In Florida, both the overall population and the 65 and over share will rise much faster than the national average. In contrast, many states will see slow growth in their populations, together with rapid aging of the population. Overall, these patterns suggest little correlation between overall population growth and the degree of population aging across states.

FAMILY STRUCTURE AND AGING

With population aging, the typical household will decline in size. Families headed by people 60 and over are 22 percent smaller than the average family.[5] The share of families with children will decline as well. In light of these patterns, relationships between older individuals and their children, grandchildren, and other relatives will undoubtedly become more complicated. The rising share of seniors may cause financial and emotional strains on families, especially if declines in family size reduce the ability for younger people to share caregiving burdens. Over the next 30 years, individuals 75 and older will increase by 83 percent, more than four times the 17 percent rise in the number of 25- to 64-year-olds.[6] On the other hand, the higher proportion of seniors might offer middle-aged parents help with child care and other services.

DEMOGRAPHIC CHANGE AND THE WORKFORCE

The mix of demographic trends will generate a workforce that will grow over the next 30 years, but at a slower rate than over the last three decades. The growth will be uneven in terms of age, race, ethnicity, location, education, and immigrant status. The 25- to 54-year-old population—often described as the prime age workforce—will decline from 44 percent to 36 percent of the total population. In a number of states, where population growth is concentrated among older people and immigration is low, the workforce will barely increase and the share of middle-age workers will decline. Other states will see expanding supplies of workers, both because of increases in births, international immigration, and internal migration. Regionally, shifts in the size of the job market will continue toward the South and West. However, the college graduate workforce may continue to expand in many cities that otherwise are experiencing little or no overall population growth (Franklin 2003).

Several demographic trends are likely to influence future educational levels of workers. Given existing patterns of educational attainment, shifts in the race and ethnicity of the population will lower the gains in the schooling levels of the overall workforce. Given the links between family structure and schooling outcomes, the continuing high levels of single parenthood might also reduce schooling levels of future workers. Population aging may well be a neutral force in affecting future educational levels of the workforce. In the last few decades, the older segments of the workforce moving into retirement had far less education than the entering cohorts of workers. As a result, education levels of the workforce increased substantially. However, the gap in education between various age groups in the workforce has narrowed, indicating that population aging might have little impact. In addition, the increasing 65 and over population might even raise educational levels of the workforce because the more educated elderly will be more likely to participate in the workforce, while those with lower education will exit the workforce.

These workforce trends will depend on policy as well as demography. The three main policy areas of major consequence for the workforce involve immigration, retirement, and education and training. Policymakers may choose to adopt a more selective immigration policy that shifts entry criteria more in the direction of the skills of the immigrant than his or her family relations in the United States. The government may provide incentives to remain in the workforce at older ages, thereby increasing the growth in the workforce. These incentives may differentially affect older workers with more education. Finally, the education and training systems may substantially improve educational outcomes of future workers, especially Hispanic-Americans, who represent a rising share of the workforce.

DEMOGRAPHIC CHANGE AND EDUCATION

Enrollment in elementary and secondary education will continue to rise in the coming years, with nearly 4.3 million additional students by 2016 (U.S. Department of Education 2007 data). Closely mirroring population trends, the projected increase is largely driven by immigration. Although fertility rates are declining among the native-born population, they remain high for immigrant families. These patterns of family formation and immigration will interact to greatly expand the proportion of Hispanic students in elementary and secondary schools. For our nation's schools, more resources will be needed to keep up with growing enrollment, particularly in the Southern and Western United States, in states and cities with the highest net in-migration.

A more diverse student body will bring with it further challenges to the U.S. education system. Schools will undoubtedly need to enhance cultural awareness and language skills for both students and parents. Parental income and education have been shown to be strong predictors of student achievement and attainment, and 40 percent of Hispanic children live with parents who lack a high school diploma or GED. The comparable figure is just 7 percent for non-Hispanic children, suggesting that overall educational attainment may decrease in the coming years. More promising, however, is that educational attainment is much higher among second and third generation Hispanics than among first generation (Suro and Passel 2003), and Asian immigrants show particularly strong patterns of educational success (Kao and Tienda 1995). Overall increases in parental education levels also work in the direction of improved educational achievement and attainment for the next generation.

Differences in family background will also bring challenges for our education system. Rising rates of divorce and single-parenthood, particularly among low-income groups, mean that this generation will grow up with less parental support than past generations. On the other hand, declining fertility rates and family size may counteract this effect. What is clear is that the growth in women's labor force participation has and will continue to put pressure on school systems to provide pre-Kindergarten and afterschool programs.

Patterns of postsecondary enrollment are much more difficult to predict than patterns of elementary and secondary education, as they only loosely correspond to population trends. As the population ages, a lower proportion of traditional college-age students will bring college attendance down. Increasing immigration may have a similar effect, if Hispanic students continue to be underrepresented on college campuses. On the other hand, the increasing enrollment of non-traditional students will exert a countervailing influence—since 1970 the number of students over age 25 has more than tripled. Putting these trends together, the U.S. Department of Education (2007) predicts an additional 2.7 million students enrolled in postsecondary education by 2016.

The labor market plays a particularly important and complicated role in college-going. As the returns to college increased for women and minorities over the last several decades, these groups enrolled in college in record numbers. Women now outnumber men on college campuses, comprising 57 percent of enrollment (U.S. Department of Education 2007). Further, postsecondary education is countercyclical. As the labor market tightens, the unemployed often go back to school to upgrade their skills or switch careers, suggesting that enrollment may surge in the months and years ahead. On the other hand, the tightening of credit markets means that many students may not be able to find loans to finance the cost of their education. In light of these patterns, two-year community colleges are likely to grow in popularity. Workers seeking vocational skills on a short time frame and students seeking inexpensive alternatives to four-year colleges are likely to turn to the nation's system of public community colleges in the years to come.

As much as demography influences education, so too does policy. Immigration policies will undoubtedly influence the number and diversity of tomorrow's students. Labor policies may have important impacts on parental work decisions and child care, as well as adult education. Finally, education finance policies will likely exert the greatest impact our nation's education system. From facilities improvements, to financial aid, the choices that policymakers make to invest in our students will shape the U.S. education system in important ways for years to come.

CONCLUSIONS

The goal of this book was to examine the implications of demographic trends for the U.S. workforce and systems of education, and in that, we hope we have succeeded. The preceding chapters have documented the sharp drop in birth rates and death rates; the shift away from married-couple households; the large-scale and diverse immigration patterns from Europe, Latin American, and Asia; the move from rural to urban areas; and a host of other demographic patterns that have shaped the destiny of the United States over the last half-century. We have explored the various ways in which these patterns have influenced and will continue to influence the U.S. workforce and our systems of education and training. From trainees to retirees, from grade school to grad school, the ever-changing faces of American workers and students reflect our country's greatest challenges as well as our greatest strengths.

NOTES

1. For the U.S. Census methodology document, see http://www.census.gov/population/www/projections/methodstatement.pdf.   For another recent and credible set of projections, see Passel and Cohn (2008).

2. All projections in this section come from the U.S. Census. See http://www.census.gov/population/www/projections/summarytables.html.

3. These figures come from the Migration Policy Institute, MPI Data Hub, http://www.migrationinformation.org/datahub/files/MPIData Hub_ACS_2007-NumberForeignBorn.xls.

4. The figures come from tabulations by authors from the March 2008 Current Population Survey.

5. U.S. Bureau of the Census, Table A2, http://www.census.gov/population/www/socdemo/hh-fam/cps2007.html.

6. Authors' tabulations based on U.S. Population Projections, Bureau of the Census, http://www.census.gov/population/www/projections/downloadablefiles.html.

REFERENCES

Ellis, Mark, and Jamie Goodwin-White. 2006. "1.5 Generation Internal Migration in the U.S.: Dispersion from States of Immigration." *International Migration Review* 40(4): 899–926.

Franklin, Rachel. 2003. "Domestic Migration across Regions, Divisions, and States, 1995–2000." Washington, DC: U.S. Bureau of the Census.

He, Wei, and Jason Schachter. 2003. *Internal Migration of the Older Population, 1995–2000.* Census 2000 Special Reports. Washington, DC: U.S. Bureau of the Census. http://www.census.gov/prod/2003pubs/censr-10.pdf.

Kao, Grace, and Marta Tienda. 1995. "Optimism and Achievement: The Educational Performance of Immigrant Youth." *Social Science Quarterly* 76(1): 1–18.

Passel, Jeffrey, and D'Vera Cohn. 2008. *U.S. Population Projections, 2005–2050.* Washington, DC: Pew Research Center. http://pewhispanic.org/files/reports/85.pdf.

Suro, Roberto, and Jeffrey S. Passel. 2003. *The Rise of the Second Generation: Changing Patterns in Hispanic Population Growth.* Washington, DC: Pew Hispanic Center and Urban Institute.

U.S. Department of Education. 2007. *Digest of Education Statistics.* Washington, DC: National Center for Education Statistics. http://nces.ed.gov/Programs/digest.

Index

ABOUT THE AUTHORS

ROBERT I. LERMAN is Senior Fellow at the Urban Institute in Washington, D.C., and professor of economics at American University. The recipient of awards for his research, he is the author or coauthor of dozens of refereed journal articles, numerous book chapters, and five books or monographs. His work deals with critical social and economic policy issues. He was one of the first scholars to examine the economic determinants of unwed fatherhood and to propose a youth apprenticeship strategy in the United States. He has been interviewed and frequently cited in the media, including NPR, Bloomberg News, the *Washington Post*, *The Economist*, and the *Financial Times*.

STEPHANIE RIEGG CELLINI is an assistant professor of public policy and economics at George Washington University. She received her M.A. and Ph.D. in economics from the University of California, Los Angeles, and her B.A. in public policy from Stanford University. Her research interests include education policy, labor economics, demography, and public finance. She is the recipient of numerous awards and fellowships and has authored several articles and book chapters. Her most recent work appears in the *Journal of Policy Analysis and Management*, *American Law and Economics Review*, *Review of Higher Education*, and *Economics of Education Review*.